"To Punky & Goody"

The old man is holding on.

Warren Brown

2-14-95

THE SOCIAL IMPACT OF THE BLACK PRESS

Dr. Warren Henry Brown

A Hearthstone Book

Carlton Press Corp.   **New York, N. Y.**

In reverence and to the eternal memory
of my beloved wife, Mattie Pearl Julian Brown.
She aided me in my research and in the total
technical development of the text from the beginning to
completion of the manuscript. I dedicate this effort to her.

CONTENTS

PREFACE

Comprehensive accounts have been written of the part played by the Black in various periods of our history, because the Black was so conspicuously involved in the political life of the periods. These accounts, however, have not dealt inclusively with the Black Press, and thus there was a missing link in the discussion of Black institutions. Since Black Newspapers both functioned in the interests of racial adjustment and reflected the social and economic life of the group, it seems that they should be considered in a comprehensive history of the group, or indeed of the nation.

By the Black Press, I mean the newspapers edited and published by Blacks. Perhaps very few persons are acquainted with the fact that Black newspapers existed in as early as pre-Civil War days.

The material was selected from the Black newspapers on the basis of their relation to the economic status of the Blacks and their struggle as free laborers, the function of the newspapers as social institutions, the types of editors and their roles of leadership, the social adjustment of the Black and the struggle for social justice.

A prologue has been written to give a historical setting of the Black in America. The reader will find evidence of the continuous rise of Blacks from a low to a higher status.

Because of the position of the Black in the nineteenth century, no special care was given to the preservation of their newspapers by libraries of the cities where they were published. This called for a long and diligent search for these newspapers.

Acknowledgement is given here to Dr. H. H. Speier for his generous assistance during the most difficult stages of this undertaking. A very grateful thanks is given to Miss Rosie K. Nelson and Mrs. Irma Julian Copper for their general assistance. Librarians everywhere are remembered for their patience and efforts to make available documents and newspapers for this book.

Warren Henry Brown

THE SOCIAL IMPACT OF THE BLACK PRESS

I. SOCIAL MOBILITY OF BLACKS

When the Black man first entered America, a people's struggle to establish a new world was just beginning. Although there are records of Blacks with some of the early explorers, the first to be settled in the United States were twenty who were brought to Jamestown, Virginia, in 1619, one year before the "Mayflower" arrived. From that early period, Blacks became the pole around which the nation's development revolved. The first chapter of the nation's history reached a climax when the cotton culture, literally rising upon the backs of Blacks in the South, threatened to defeat the noble experiment in social and political democracy. As indentured servants, and later as slaves, Blacks kept alive the root of feudalism in the South and formed the bedrock of four distinct classes: the Black laborers, the "poor whites," small businessmen, and the plantation masters.[1]

> Research has proved that the first Negroes . . . and others brought by early privateers were not reduced to slavery, but to limited servitude, a legalized status of Indian, white and Negro servants preceding slavery in most, if not all, of the English mainland colonies . . .[2]

The system of slavery did not develop until later. Indeed the development was so gradual that it was in existence before it was recognized. Massachusetts legalized the system in 1641,

---

[1]W. E. B. DuBois, *Black Reconstruction in America* (New York: Harcourt, Brace & Co., 1934), p. 37.

[2]*The New International Encyclopedia* (New York: Dodd, Mead, & Co., 1916.) Now published by Funk & Wagnalls Co., XXI, p. 166.

Connecticut in 1650, Virginia in 1661, and the other colonies later, Georgia not until 1749, though slavery was in effect there long before given this legal sanction. By the year 1775 slavery had been introduced into every known territory in North America from Canada to Florida.

The system of slavery had not been allowed to develop unchallenged. As early as 1688 the German Quakers of Germantown, Pennsylvania, led by Francis Daniel Pastorius, had made a formal protest against this traffic in human beings. Elsewhere groups and individuals had raised moral objections to the enslavement of any people. Various colonies, from 1695 on, had tried to stop the trade by imposing duties or passing laws, but both the trade and slavery itself had been found profitable and, therefore, these regulations carried little weight. During the Revolutionary period the system of slavery tended to decline. This decline was due, in part, to the general humanitarian movement that was awakening both America and Europe. It was due in part also to the spread of liberal ideas, which culminated in the French Revolution, in various reforms in England, and in our own Revolution. In the course of all the discussion of the rights of man and the freedom of the individual it was natural that some consideration should be given to the plight of those men and women who were being deprived of the ordinary rights of human beings.

When the Declaration of Independence was being formulated, therefore, and even up to the time of its ratification, there was hope of bringing slavery to an end.[3] Failure of the document to achieve this end caused Thomas Jefferson, it is said, to lament over the crisis that the problem of slavery would eventually precipitate. Thus a possible opportunity for establishing citizenship rights for Blacks passed.

Some slight change in the attitudes of a few people was made by the fact that Blacks to the number of three thousand fought in the Continental army. New York, Rhode Island, and Virginia freed those slaves who had served as soldiers. The system as a whole, though, was not shaken by these manumissions.

When the Constitution was being framed there was some

---

[3]W. E. B. DuBois, *The Negro* (New York: Henry Holt & Co., 1915), p. 193.

agitation for the abolition of the slave trade. It was finally agreed that after twenty years, in 1808, the trade, but not the institution of slavery, should cease. Before the slave trade was outlawed, and indeed before the end of the Revolutionary period, northern and middle states began passing laws leading to emancipation of Blacks. Rhode Island was the first state to take this course, when it put a ban on slavery by passing a law in 1774 that stated that all children born of slave mothers were to be free. The state of Massachusetts outlawed slavery in 1780, and four years later Connecticut took a similar step. Shortly thereafter, Pennsylvania, Virginia, Maryland, New Hampshire, New York, and New Jersey adopted abolition measures.

Economic factors were responsible for the fact that in spite of all the moral arguments against it the system of slavery was permitted to develop. Economic factors were responsible also for the fact that slavery became more firmly rooted in some sections of the country than in others. There was wealth in the New World, but labor was necessary to procure it. In a country where everyone could have land of their own, no one had any desire or any need to work for another. The only labor available, therefore, was forced labor. Consequently the moral arguments against the holding of Black slaves were ineffectual, and Blacks were imported in large numbers.

The Black man was the pioneer in the hard physical work that began the reduction of the American wilderness and which not only hastened the economic development of America directly but indirectly released for other employment thousands of white men and thus enabled America to grow economically and spiritually at a rate previously unparalleled in history. It was Black labor that established the modern world commerce which began first as a commerce in the bodies of the slaves themselves and was the primary cause of the prosperity of the first great commercial cities of our day. Then Black labor was thrown into the production of four great crops—tobacco, sugar, rice and cotton. These crops were not new but their production on a large cheap scale was new and had a special significance because they catered to the demands of the masses of men and thus made

13

possible an interchange of goods such as the luxury trade of the Middle Ages catering to the rich could not build. . . .[4]

The economic value of Blacks became increasingly important after the beginning of the Industrial Revolution in Europe, which had its influence in America as well. The Black, an unlimited source of labor, became the machine that laid the groundwork for America's leading industries.

The greatest concentration of slaves was found in the South and the Southwest. This condition was due not to the moral character of the settlers in those sections but to the fact that the South and the Southwest had soil, climate, and character of land suitable for the four great crops: tobacco, sugar, rice, and cotton. All of these crops needed vast tracts of land, and therefore large numbers of laborers. A seemingly unlimited supply of land was available, but no free labor in large numbers; and anyway free labor would have been too costly, since before the crops could be even started virgin land had to be cleared. Therefore thousands and thousands of slaves were purchased.

Of the four great crops for which cheap labor was essential, cotton became more widely cultivated than any of the others, and was largely responsible for the perpetuation of slavery, and for the reopening of the slave trade after 1808, the date set for it to be outlawed. The invention of the cotton gin and the steamboat, which made the production and export of cotton vastly more profitable than hitherto, made Blacks indispensable to the cotton culture. Instead of social conditions of the Blacks being gradually improved, as had seemed possible near the close of the eighteenth century, slave regulations became severer, in order that the economic order might be safeguarded. The slave trade did not cease in 1808, though after that date it was carried on without the sanction of the law. More cotton meant more slaves and more slaves meant more cotton, until eventually almost all the economic energy of the South and Southwest was being expended on this one crop.

Blacks in America increased by 200,000 during the ten-year

---

[4]W. E. B. DuBois, *The Gift of Black Folk* (Boston: Stratford Pub. Co., 1924), pp. 52-53.

period ending in 1800, by 300,000 in the next decade, but by 500,000 in the decade ending in 1830.[5] "Bootlegging" of slaves was carried on even after the Civil War had started. The price of an adult male increased from $200 in 1800 to $1400-$2000 in 1860.

At the same time the cotton production increased from 200,000 pounds in 1790 to 35,600,000 pounds in 1800. Thereafter it about doubled each decade, until 1860 it totaled 1,820,708,000 pounds, and made up 57 per cent of the value of the total export of the country.

With this tremendous increase in cotton culture and the urgent need for Black free labor, a defense of the institution of slavery grew up. In order to justify this defense there developed also the doctrine of racial inferiority and superiority.

Just as soil, climate, and character of land were the determinants in the fastening of slavery on the South and the Southwest, so were they the determinants in the early outlawing of slavery in the North. How natural forces influenced the kind of society that developed in the North is suggested by James Morgan in these words:

An unreconstructed southerner once lamented that Plymouth Rock did not fall on the Pilgrim Fathers. Millions of Plymouth rocks did land on the men who came to found a landed aristocracy in New England . . . and turned them into Yankee traders. The glacier that strewed Massachusetts with boulders was a great democrat. The Puritan aristocrats could not carve baronial estates out of such a stingy soil or have a servile class to sweat for them. Those stony fields never could be cleared by indentured Negro slaves, but only by men working for themselves.

New England was an economic democracy, a democracy at the bottom, because by the time a man had rolled the stones off a patch of ground, the lean earth would yield him only enough to keep him and his family. There was nothing left for an idle landlord.[6]

[5]Edwin R. Embree, *Brown America* (New York: Viking Press, 1921), p. 16.

[6]James Morgan, *The Birth of the American People* (New York: Macmillan & Co., 1930), p. 98.

In the North it was for the most part through trade that the Black had an effect upon the economic life. First of all, it was largely ships from the northern colonies, where farming did not prove profitable, that entered the slave-carrying trade. Fortunes were built on this trade, the center of which in the early days was Newport, Rhode Island. Long after slavery itself had been abolished in the New England states, slaves were still sent out from some of her ports. Slavery also influenced these trading colonies indirectly, for, to a great extent it was through her ports that the products of slave labor passed.

When the slave trade was reopened, after 1808, it was New England and New York that reaped the greatest profits from the illicit trade. It was said that in New York "downtown merchants of wealth and respectability" carried on the buying and selling of Blacks with comparatively little interruption, "and that during eighteen months of 1859–1860 eighty slavers were fitted out in that city."[7] Massachusetts and Portland, Maine, were almost as important in this traffic as was New York.

Before the African trade had to any extent been reopened, however, the increased demand for laborers had been met by the Middle States—Virginia, Maryland, and Kentucky. This section had long been the center of a domestic slave-trade. Slaves could not be used there in large numbers; consequently the surplus slaves were sold farther south. Francis Higginson writing in 1834 said that six thousand were being sent out of Virginia annually to southern or western markets.[8]

Although slavery was permitted to develop in the United States, and as its economic value increased was even hotly defended, still not all the Blacks in the United States were slaves. When the first census was taken, in 1790, there were 59,584 free Blacks in the country and 697,624 slaves. By 1869 the slave population had risen to 3,949,557, and the free Black population to 550,000. Chart 1 shows graphically the rise in Black slaves as compared with the rise in free Blacks. From

[7]W. E. B. DuBois, *The Suppression of the African Slave-Trade to the United States of America* (Cambridge, Mass.: Harvard University Press, 1896), pp. 178-179.

[8]Francis John Higginson, *Remarks on Slavery and Emancipation* (Boston: Hilliard, Gray and Company, 1834), pp. 15-16.

Chart 1: NEGRO POPULATION UNTITED STATES SLAVES—FREE 1790-1860

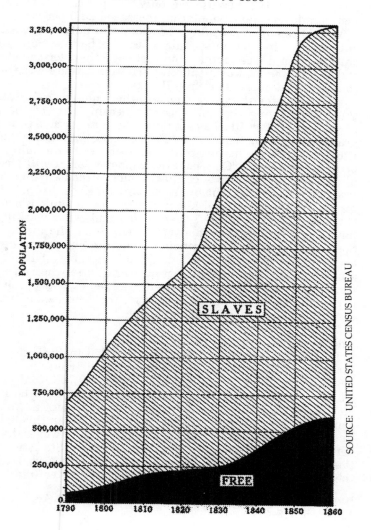

1820 to 1830 the free colored population increased at a rate of 36.2 per cent. Then came a period of decline, so that for the next ten years the increase was only 20.4 per cent. During this last decade the slave population increased 23.5 per cent.

Most of this increase of free Blacks was a natural growth. A child born of free parents would, of course, be free. So would a child born of a free mother and a slave father, for the child's status followed that of the mother. However, there were other causes for the increase of free Blacks.

When new territory was added to the Union as a free state, the Blacks living therein of course became part of the free population. A few Blacks came into the country as free immigrants, such being listed in the 1860 census. Sometimes a slave was freed because he had rendered a service to an individual or to a community. Occasionally a master left a will freeing all his slaves. Hundreds of Blacks had purchased their own freedom, or been bought by friends or relatives. Francis Higginson (1834) stated that about a third of the adult Blacks in Cincinnati had redeemed themselves and were working to have their friends and relatives freed. Since the aim of the South was to protect its economic structure by continuing the slave institution, the only considerable number of Blacks to gain their freedom in that section were those who ran away from their masters. Some hundreds escaped by way of the Underground Railroad, the term used for the concerted activities to help to safety those who ran away.

The Economic Status of the Free Black

To a large extent the free Blacks settled in the cities. For instance, in 1830 there was the following distribution: Boston 1,875; New York, 14,083; Philadelphia, 9,796; Baltimore, 14,790; Charleston, 2,106; New Orleans, 11,906. In both the North and the South the free Black was important as an artisan, but in the North he gradually lost his hold in this field as immigrant labor displaced him. In the South, however, he had very little competition until after the Civil War. Statistics from the census of 1850 show the contrast in this respect between the North and the South: [9] New York had twelve free Black

---

[9]Phillips, *American Negro Slavery* (New York: D. Appleton Co., 1918), pp. 438-439.

carpenters and no masons; New Orleans had in these trades 355 and 278, respectively. The two cities had a similar proportion of tailors, painters, coopers, blacksmiths and general mechanics. In New Orleans only one tenth of the free Blacks were in unskilled work, and no men were listed as domestics. A number of free Blacks in the South became independent farmers. A few in the South and a considerable number in the North went into business. By 1860 free Blacks of New Orleans had acquired property valued at $15,000,000; in 1856 those of New England were reported as having property and business worth $2,000,000; in Ohio, Illinois, and Michigan, $1,500,000; in New York and Pennsylvania, $3,000,000.[10]

Carter Woodson says that the Blacks as a group had their best economic opportunity in Cincinnati. He gives the following examples of progressive individuals who belonged to this group:

By 1840 the Negroes of this city had acquired $228,000 of real estate. One Negro was worth $6,000; another who had purchased himself for $5,000 a few years prior to 1840, was worth $1,000. Another Negro paid $5,000 for himself and his family and bought a home worth $800 to $1,000. A freedman who was a slave until he was twenty-four years of age, then had two lots worth $10,000, paid a tax of $40, and had 320 acres of land in Mercer County, Ohio . . . A woman who was a slave until she was thirty then had property worth $2,000 . . . Another Negro, who had been on the auction block in 1832, had spent $2,600 purchasing himself and his family. He had bought two brick houses valued at $6,000, and 560 acres of land in Mercer County, Ohio said to be worth $2,500.[11]

Black Manhattan gives us a brief account of this place, which was for generations the most famous tavern in New York City:

---

[10]Willis D. Weatherford and Charles S. Johnson, *Race Relations*, New York: (D. C. Heath and Company, 1934), pp. 255-256.

[11]Carter G. Woodson, *The Negro in Our History* (Washington D.C.: The Association for the Study of Negro Life and History, 1928), pp. 259-260.

It was established by Samuel Fraunces, a colored man from an island of the French West Indies . . . Fraunces bought the property in 1762 for two thousand pounds. It was at Fraunces's Tavern that the body now known as the New York Chamber of Commerce was organized, in 1768. The inn was frequented by General Washington, and it was there that he bade farewell to his officers, on December 4, 1783. The farewell dinner was tendered by Governor Clinton . . . Fraunces personally conducted the tavern for a number of years. He was well known and well liked by the most prominent New York citizens of his day. His daughter, Phoebe, was Washington's housekeeper at the mansion which the Commander-in-Chief occupied as headquarters in New York in 1776. When Washington became President he made Fraunces steward of what was then the White House, in New York, located at Number 3, Cherry Street. He remained in Washington's employ in New York and Philadelphia until 1786 or later, as shown by receipts signed by Fraunces, one of which is now on exhibition, at the tavern.

Fraunces's Tavern was purchased and restored as a memorial, in 1905, by the Sons of the Revolution.[12]

Legal Status of the Free Black

The legal status of the free Blacks varied from time to time and place to place. During colonial times their position was not much different from that of the free whites. In all the colonies except Georgia, South Carolina, and Virginia they were permitted to vote. South Carolina disfranchised them in 1716; Virginia in 1723; and Georgia in 1761. After the Revolution, for a few years at least, there was a tendency to interpret literally the declaration: "all men are created equal" and "endowed" with the "inalienable rights of life, liberty and the pursuit of happiness." Gradually, however, the rights of even the free Blacks were restricted. It was difficult to find arguments to justify slavery if in the same communities where some Blacks were held as slaves others had all the rights and

---

[12]James W. Johnson, *Black Manhattan* (New York: Alfred A. Knopf, 1930), pp. 44–45.

privileges of free citizens. In most parts of the middle west there was no discrimination against Blacks while these sections were territories, but after they were admitted as states they passed disfranchising laws. Blacks voted in Louisiana until 1812; in North Carolina as late as 1835; Arkansas, 1836; and Texas, 1845. Ohio disfranchised them as early as 1803; Kansas, not until 1836. Rhode Island at first permitted them to vote, then took away this privilege, but in 1842 gave it back. In New York, Blacks could vote, but had to pass a special property qualification. Maine, New Hampshire, and Vermont had a property qualification, but it was the same for all voters.

Education Before 1860

Before 1860 Blacks had made commendable advances in education. Some had acquired formal training for the professions; public schools had been established in the free states, and free Negroes in some of the other sections were having their children privately educated; there were two institutions of higher learning: Lincoln University in Pennsylvania, and Wilberforce, in Ohio.

All in all, it is evident, as Benjamin Brawley says, in *A Social History of the American Black*, "that honorable achievement on the part of the Blacks and general advances in social welfare by no means began with the Emancipation Proclamation. In 1860 eight-ninths of the race were still slaves, but in face of every possible handicap the one-ninth that was free entered practically every field of human endeavor."[13]

The slaves, of course, supplied the huge labor force needed in the cotton culture. The slave population could not be isolated from the "poor whites" in their economic relationship, for the "poor whites," too, were despised and held in contempt by the middle class. Because of their limited number, they were not important as a source of labor to do the work performed by Blacks, but functioned in the plantation system as henchmen for the upper class. The lower middle class, some of whom owned a small number of slaves themselves, were frequently engaged by the masters to manage the plantations.

---

[13]*A Social History of the American Negro* (New York: The Macmillan Company, 1931), p. 251.

Of far more importance for the continuation of the cotton culture was the leisure class, the southern gentleman.

... Their number was comparatively small. The census of 1860 put the white population of the slave states at 8,099,760 and the slaves at 3,953,580; the slaves were owned by only 384,000 whites, of whom 107,957 owned more than ten, 10,781 owned fifty or more, but 1,733 owned 100 or more.... Around 1850 ... a thousand families received $50,000,000 a year, while the remaining 660,000 families received only $60,000,000, a concentration of wealth and income hardly surpassed in the most advanced stage of an industrial society.[14]

They were lord and master, for in their hands were vested the vast agricultural land and labor of the South. Since the ownership of property was necessary to qualify an individual for political office in most of the Southern states, planters elected one from among their class to hold all such positions.[15] Representation in Congress and in state assemblies included "poor whites" and Blacks, but planters voted for them; thus the political strength of two hundred and seventy planters prior to 1860 represented from one to two million votes as compared with the vote of free men in the North.

The planters as a whole were more interested in leisure-time activities and luxuries than in supervising their plantations. To secure more money for their pleasures, they increased their production of cotton. With more money they engaged in even less work and indulged in more luxuries. This desire on the part of the planters for more and more leisure and more and more luxuries led to an overexpansion, and then the breakdown, of the cotton culture.

Land and slave property in 1860 were assessed at a value of $5,000,000,000.[16] In other words, about one third of the country's money was invested in Blacks,[17] but the return from the

[14]Harold Underwood Faulkner, *American Political and Social History* (New York: F. S. Crofts & Co., 1941), p. 285.

[15]DuBois, *Black Reconstruction in America*, p. 32.

[16]Edward F. Humphrey, *An Economic History of the United States* (New York: The Century Co., 1931), p. 270.

[17]*Ibid.*

investment was an insignificant figure, amounting to less than $300,000,000 during the peak of the cotton production. Yet the planters, before the inevitable turn of events, used what income they did get to indulge in luxuries and to purchase more slaves.[18]

The disintegration of the leisure class and the overexpansion of cotton planting were contributing causes to the breakdown of the cotton culture. Another cause was the lack of rotation of crops. Though the soil was rich, its fertility needed to be conserved, and rotation of crops was essential for this conservation. But no thought was given to the future fertility of the soil. The one thought was for more and more cotton. Still another factor that contributed to the breakdown of the cotton culture was the lack of scientific training of the slaves. They were not trained to use equipment and improvements instituted by the Industrial Revolution. Notwithstanding the fact that most of the skilled laborers of the South prior to 1860 were Black, many planters failed to realize this situation, and seemed to feel that the slaves could not be trained to use machinery. More important was the fact that planters were afraid to train Blacks. They felt that if they improved the efficiency of their slaves this might give them ideas of independence and lead to insurrection.

The breakdown of the cotton culture led to the crisis ending in the Civil War. Fundamentally, the question to be decided was whether the nation was to expand as an agricultural or as an industrial civilization.[19] Under the domination of the small farmers, the North had gradually become an industrial community. The small farmers were organized to increase production and consumption on a sound financial basis. They considered slave labor as an unfair weapon of competition, and they were constantly urging Congress to act in behalf of free labor. Thus economic factors brought political action to the front, as there was an attempt to reach an agreement between the agriculturist and the industrialist in regard to labor. In 1854, the Kansas-Nebraska Act, which gave settlers in new

---

[18]*Ibid.*
[19]*Ibid.*, p. 269.

territory the right to decide for themselves the question of slavery, attempted to reconcile the conflicting groups.

This legislative effort on the slave question failed, however, to satisfy both sections, for the Dred Scott decision, handed down by Chief Justice Roger Taney of the United States Supreme Court, was an upset to a possibility of temporary peace. In 1857, the Chief Justice decreed that a slave was the private property of the owner, and a runaway slave found in free territory had to be returned to his master. The court's action was interpreted by Northerners as creating an illegal situation, and many of them defied the ruling.

Quite naturally, the major political parties shifted their platforms around the subject of slavery. The Democrats could not avert a break in their party line, for some were bent on the unlimited expansion of slavery. Perhaps this split among the Democrats led to Republican victory.

Abraham Lincoln was the Republicans' standard bearer, and his election to the presidency of the United States brought about the beginning of secession from the Union. Obviously, Lincoln's proposals of compromise were not acceptable to the agricultural South, for his declaration of government was in opposition to his philosophy. Southerners could not reconcile Lincoln's pledge, "My paramount object in this struggle is to save the Union and not to save or destroy slavery," and his expressed desire, "I certainly wish all men could be free." During his campaign Lincoln was characterized by his opponents as an evasive person not to be trusted. Animosity between the North and South was further stirred by propagandists who circulated reports that Lincoln advocated intermarriage between the Blacks and whites.

After Lincoln's election, one newspaper announced:

. . . The time has come; Lincoln has been elected—the curtain has risen and the first act of the dark drama of Black Republicanism has been reached—the issue has been boldly met—throw doubt and indecision to the winds—the requisite steps should be taken at once for the arming and equipment of every able-bodied man—the irrepressible conflict has commenced—we must meet it manfully and bravely—Florida will secede.[20]

The southern states' resistance to industrial culture was based on the rationalization that Black slave labor could be used as efficiently as the paid labor of the North and of Europe.[21] The truth of the matter was that the giving up of Black labor would have meant a sacrifice of income and would have necessitated the planters' devoting more time to their business.[22] Thus the leisure class preferred to advocate the superiority of Black labor because it was to their economic benefit to do so. Also

... The espousal of the doctrine of Negroes' inferiority by the South was primarily because of economic motives, and the inter-connected political urge necessary to support the slave industry, but to the watching world it sounded like the carefully thought out result of experience and reason.[23]

The general sentiment in the North concerning slavery was divided into two groups. One group advocated the abolition of slavery and also urged full citizenship for Blacks, whereas the other group wanted merely to eliminate the economic evil by freeing the slaves, but were not concerned about the Blacks' political and legal rights. When the northern army marched southward, however, it was not in protest against slavery, but in defense of the new economic system. No further compromise was possible between the old and new economies.

The war, during the first year and a half, caused severe difficulties for the Union armies. Their forces were repelled at all points and public opinion in the North urging the President to emancipate slaves as a weapon against the Confederates took on momentous force. Military sanctions under the

---

[20]William W. Davis, *The Civil War and Reconstruction in Florida*, p. 47.
[21]DuBois, *Black Reconstruction in America*, p. 39.
[22]*Ibid.*
[23]*Ibid.*

changed conditions rested upon the President.[25] On that authority, he would not consider the seceded states as his enemies, nor would he regard them as ever having been a separate entity. His plan was to admit a state back into the Union when ten per cent of those who had voted in 1860 had taken an oath of allegiance to the Union and organized a state government, and when the state had ratified the Thirteenth Amendment. Thus the President began his task by attempting to establish a "loyalty class" within each southern state. Under the protection of the army, this class was to be delegated with the responsibility of directing the political functions of the several states according to Union principles.[26] The President was of the opinion that ten per cent was a sufficient number to inculcate democratic principles into the majority of the people. On this point, Lincoln's idea has been challenged,[27] for a minority can control the majority only when it is strong enough to shift the balance of power. Certainly such a condition did not exist.

The main issue of the campaign to re-elect Lincoln was based upon his Reconstruction views. Whatever his full program might have been, he avoided serious breaks with his political adherents and was elected President for a second term. Shortly thereafter, April 5, 1865, he succumbed to an assassin's bullet, and the political phase of Reconstruction was made more difficult.

Lincoln's successor, Andrew Johnson, promised to follow Lincoln's plan for Reconstruction. Johnson, however, lacked courage, astuteness, and vision to carry out the tremendous undertaking that Lincoln had begun. Since the new President was a Southerner, he became the symbol of hope for the "poor whites" of the South, and the fusion of the North and the South became more difficult.

Under the presidential plan of Reconstruction all the states had complied with the terms and were ready to be admitted to the Union by 1866. The legislatures in many of the states,

---

[25]John Burgess, *Reconstruction and the Constitution* (New York: C. Scribner's Sons, 1902), p. 9.

[26]*Ibid.*

[27]*Ibid.*

however, had enacted laws dealing with the Black, which became known as the "Black codes," and which made Congress feel that the Black was in danger of again being enslaved. Congress, therefore, refused to readmit these states and took over the responsibility of Reconstruction. The southern states were divided into five military districts, each directed by a general. State conventions were to be held for the purpose of drawing up new state constitutions. Elections to the conventions were to take place under the supervision of army officers, with Blacks voting, but certain leaders of the Confederacy not voting. The state constitutions were compelled to provide for Black suffrage, and the Fourteenth Amendment, which provided for the civil and legal rights of the Black, had to be ratified by the states. Between 1868 and 1871 all the seceded states had been taken back into the Union. In the meantime they had also ratified the Fifteenth Amendment, which provided for Black suffrage.

The constitutional conventions were composed of "scalawags" (southern "poor whites"), northern carpetbaggers, swindlers and racketeers, and Blacks. In the South Carolina convention the Blacks outnumbered the whites; in the Louisiana convention the two groups were equal.

Among the first states to undertake the adjustment necessary to gain federal recognition was Louisiana. Louisiana's reconstruction marked, for the first time in the United States, an ideal political democracy as far as the position of the Black was concerned. Blacks asserted their power in exercising their right to vote and it was the only state ever to elect a Black to the office of lieutenant-governor. The state was, however, the scene of political party wars and rioting because of conflict among Republicans, and hostilities between Republicans and Democrats. The crux of all the conflicts, regardless of party label, was political rights of Blacks. The intrigues within political parties will be considered at greater length in a subsequent chapter.

The southern states, although they apparently accepted the terms of the Congressional Reconstruction, were not reconciled to the new order. Even before the last state was readmitted to the Union, the South had become active in reducing the effectiveness of legislation by organizing a wave of terror

27

against the Blacks. Such secret orders as the Regulators, Jay-hawkers, Black-horse Cavalry, and the Ku Klux Klan were organized to suppress actions on the part of Blacks and movements by whites on behalf of Blacks. A report to Congress by an officer of the Union army explained their activity. The statement read in part as follows:

> . . . I am unaware of a single instance in which one of these villains has been arrested and brought to trial by the civil authorities. . . . I am led to believe that, in some instances, the civil authorities and well disposed citizens have been over-awed by these organizations. . . . Whenever they have neglected or refused to act, troops have been dispatched to arrest the guilty parties; but, as the outlaws are usually well mounted, have the sympathy of more or less of the inhabitants, are familiar with the country, and have numerous opportunities for concealment, they generally escape.[28]

The Ku Klux Klan began its activities in 1868, and through terrorizing kept both Blacks and carpetbaggers away from the polls. After 1874 nearly all the Blacks in the lower South were prevented by persuasion, force, fraud, or new constitutions from influencing any southern election. Actual disfranchisement, however, did not begin until 1890, when Mississippi adopted a literacy test for prospective voters which required them to read or "understand" a part of the Constitution. Other states adopted a similar test or other requirements designed to apply to Blacks but not to Whites. Some states had a property qualification or made the payment of poll tax a prerequisite for voting. In some states the voting laws included a "grandfather clause"—only those were permitted to vote whose grandfathers were voting in 1860.

Congress made one attempt to prevent the illegal disfranchisement of the Black by introducing in 1899 the Lodge Bill, to provide federal supervisors at elections. The bill was defeated, however, by eight Republicans, who bargained with Democrats for support on a pending silver bill.

---

[28]W. L. Fleming, *Documentary History of the United States* (Cleveland: The Arthur H. Clark Co., 1906), p. 360.

After the Civil War the Blacks faced a serious economic situation—so serious that some whites and some Blacks advocated the creation of a state in some foreign province of the United States for the colonization of Blacks.[29] The social and economic system that had controlled the lives of the Blacks had suddenly and completely broken down. The new conditions placed upon them the responsibility of providing for themselves, and they had had practically no experience in managing their own affairs or competing with skilled workmen or other free agents. Thousands wandered around homeless, ragged, hungry, and jobless. The difficulty they experienced in making some kind of economic adjustment was aggravated by the southern whites who had no desire or willingness to consider hiring free Black labor. They did not believe in it and refused to give it a trial.

Another serious obstacle to the solution of the Black's economic problem in the South was the disastrous influence of the carpetbaggers. Greely describes them as being, in truth,

. . . a mournful fact. They are fellows who crawl down South in the track of our armies, generally at a very safe distance in the rear. . . . They ingratiate themselves with the Blacks, simple, credulous, ignorant men, very glad to be welcome and follow any whites who profess to be the champion of their rights. Some of them were elected Senators, others Representatives, some sheriffs, judges, and so on; and there they were in the public eye, stealing and plundering, many of them with both arms around Negroes and their hands in their rear pockets, seeing if they can pick a paltry dollar out of them.[30]

However, the freedmen began gradually to find a way out of

---

[29]Even today some racial sociologists suggest the creation of a separate state for all Blacks in the United States, and occasionally someone like Marcus Garvey proposes the colonization of Blacks in Africa. In 1918, Garvey founded "The Back to Africa Movement" under the auspices of the Universal Improvement Association.

[30]Horace Greeley, *Mr. Greeley's Record on Questions of Amnesty and Reconstruction from the Hour of General Lee's Surrender* (New York: 1871). A twenty-four page pamphlet.

the economic chaos. To help them adjust themselves to a free society, the Freedmen's Bureau, established during the last year of the war to handle all problems connected with the freed slaves, now had its life extended by act of Congress. The Bureau supplied Blacks with food and clothing and aided them in finding jobs. Many of them, after having been idle and bewildered for months, returned to domestic or agricultural occupations, often for their former masters, but now for wages. Many others left the farms, to find their way into the lumber and turpentine industries of the South, or to enter the steel and iron plants and the tobacco factories. Thousands rushed to the coal and iron mines of Alabama and Tennessee, and to the coal mines of Ohio and West Virginia. There was a demand for workers to build railroads in various sections of the country, and several thousand Blacks left the South to do this work. Soon employment agencies were opened in the border states and in some sections of the South to take care of the demand for laborers that began to come in from different parts of the country. Also labor agents went throughout the South encouraging Blacks to leave the cotton belt.

Once the Blacks started leaving the cotton belt there was a movement to the far South and the West. In 1879 there was such a sudden rush to the West that it was called the "Black Exodus." In 1880 it was reported that 60,000 of the migrants had settled in Kansas. When the landowners of the South, who at first had been reluctant to use free Black labor, now saw that they were losing their labor supply, they took steps to stop the migration. They called conferences to get at the reasons for the exodus. They employed varying methods from persuasion to force to stop it. But the movement away from the cotton belt continued. Intermittently it continued down to the present day, with several periods of great migration. For the most part the trend has been from rural to urban sections and corresponds with the trend that the population in general has been taking.

The importance of Black labor to both North and South was dramatically demonstrated during World War I. The new demand for workers in war industries and the recall of thousands of aliens to fight for their own countries created a labor shortage. At the same time there was failure of cotton crops in the South, and general unrest growing out of dissatisfaction with social conditions there. Thousands of Blacks, therefore, were ready to respond to the call from the industrial centers when it came. The demand for Black labor was actually started in 1915, when some Black college students were used on tobacco farms in Connecticut during the summer. Some of the growers decided to import a few families so that they could have workers all the year. Then in 1916 the Pennsylvania Railroad sent for thousands to work on their roadbeds. Many of these soon left to go into better paying jobs in the mills of Pennsylvania. Letters were sent to the people "back home" describing the North as a "land of freedom and plenty." These reports were confirmed by labor agents who came seeking workers for the various industrial concerns. The wages offered per day were sometimes more than the agricultural laborer had been getting per week.

With such inducements in the North a stream of labor turned in that direction. The stream became a torrent as the movement reached mass proportions, and exhibited all the hysteria of a mass movement. Labor agents, the Negro press, letters from the first adventurers in the North . . . churned enthusiasm to the point of heedless emotional precipitation. The Negroes, under this new stimulation, moved and gave their reasons for it afterward. Some of the migrants had felt social grievances; others had been adjusted to their positions and were moved only by the prospect of bettering their economic lot.

The towns were the first to feel the effect. There, the "pass rider"—that is, the labor agent—could move about more freely. People in the towns lived in closer contact, and news circulated more rapidly. The newspapers came in regularly, and the Negroes themselves could observe large numbers of the migrants as they left. On Saturday, the market day, when the country folk came to town they could not escape this excitement, and soon began to share it. Not only the adventurous youth suddenly quit the quiet isolation of the farm, but sturdy dependable farmers, whose lives had been spent on the farm, could not resist the temptation. . . .[31]

[31]Weatherford and Johnson, *Race Relations*, pp. 336-337.

Thousands in the towns or on the farms responded to the excitement and left their homes. Those who could do so sold their possessions; others did not wait to dispose of their houses and land—they just walked away from them. Trains could not accommodate the crowds that gathered at the stations. Some of the people waited days for labor agents to bring them passes. It is not known how many people migrated during this period, but estimates vary from 150,000 to 400,000.

Between 1921 and 1924 another migration occurred. In the South again there had been a failure of cotton crops. In the North there was a labor shortage, the result of the passing of the immigration exclusion acts. This time there was not the hysteria that had accompanied and encouraged the exodus of the war period; but though the movement was quiet, hundreds of thousands took part in it. In fact, it is estimated that during this migration 1,000,000 Blacks left the rural South. Some of the migrants settled in southern cities; the greater number, however, moved to cities in the North.

Again, just as in 1879, there was alarm on the part of the plantation owners and other employers, who saw their labor supply dwindling. Again, various methods, from persuasion to force, were used to keep the labor supply where it was. But these methods were no more successful than they had been previously. Improved conditions of wages, housing, and schools did not keep a few Blacks from joining the exodus, but on the whole the movement to the cities continued.

Blacks in smaller or larger numbers found their way into most of the industries of the country—iron and steel mills, stockyards, railroad maintenance and repair, automobile manufacturing, textile industry, construction, and a great variety of other fields. They entered skilled and semi-skilled as well as unskilled occupations.

The Bureau of Conciliation of the United States Department of Labor in 1923 canvassed 273 firms for figures on the distribution and assimilation of the migrants, and found 60,421 new Negro workers of whom 14,951 were doing skilled work and 45,470 unskilled work. During the single year September 1, 1922, to August 31, 1923, 18,050 new workers had been added to the payrolls, of which number 4,157 were skilled. The general increase in skilled workers was 38.5 per cent; of the unskilled 44.0. Some states showed an increase in skilled Negroes as high as 186.8 per cent. . . .[32]

The increase of Black workers in some of the industries was remarkable. Westinghouse Electric and Manufacturing Company in 1916, for instance, had 25 Blacks in its employ; in 1918 it had 1500. The Carnegie Steel Company of Pittsburgh had 1500 in 1916; 4000 in 1918. In the stockyards of Chicago there were 39 Blacks in 1910; in 1920 there were 5,300. Before the migration of World War I the industries of Detroit had scarcely any Blacks; in 1922 over 500 plants there were employing Blacks. Similar increases could have been reported for other centers and other industries, for the number of Blacks in industries gradually increased up to the beginning of the depression of 1929.

Of the many phases of the history of the American people none is filled with more dramatic experiences and impelling interest than that dealing with the struggles of the Negro to obtain an education. . . .[33]

After the Black was disfranchised, he "no longer sought salvation in politics and legislative measures. Education he recognized as the means to redemption and he was making immense sacrifices to secure it."[34]

There had been some education of Blacks even in the colonial period, mainly enough to enable some of them to read the Bible, in order that the church might bring them to Christianity. For a while it was customary to free any Black who was baptized. Later, however, objections to freeing these Blacks were raised and for a while it seemed that baptism and therefore teaching

[32]Charles S. Johnson, *The Negro in American Civilization* (New York: Henry Holt & Co., 1930), p. 33.

[33]Ambrose Caliver, *Education of Negro Teachers*, National Survey of the Education of Negro Teachers, Vol. IV (Washington, D.C., United States Government Printing Office, 1933), p. 1.

[34]Paul Herman Buck, *Road to Reunion* (Boston: Little Brown & Co., 1937), p. 290.

of Blacks would be stopped. But several of the colonies passed laws stating that baptism was not necessarily a cause for manumission, and so the religious groups resumed their teaching.

So far as we know, the first formal education of Negroes in America was undertaken by the Society for the Propagation of the Gospel in Foreign Parts, at Goose Creek, South Carolina. Reverend Samuel Thomas, the first missionary sent to the Negroes . . . in his first report claimed "he had taken much pains in instructing the Negroes, and had learned twenty of them to read." In his report of 1705 he wrote: "I have here presumed to give an account of one thousand slaves as far as they know of it and are desirous of Christian knowledge and seem willing to prepare themselves for it, in learning to read, for which they redeem the time from their labor. Many of them can read the Bible distinctly and great numbers of them were learning when I left the province."

Through the influence of the Society for the Propagation of the Gospel in Foreign Parts a second school was opened, in New York City in 1704, under the direction of Elias Neau. This man went from house to house and succeeded in getting a few masters to send their slaves to him for instruction. When the Negro riot of 1712 broke out in New York, it came near to wrecking this school, but it was finally proved that the leaders of the riot never received instruction in the school. The governor then gave it his protection and recommended that masters have their slaves instructed. Neau taught until his death in 1722, but there were some masters who continued to fear that training "would be a means to make the slaves more cunning and apter to wickedness." One of Neau's successors, Mr. Auckmutty, who served in the school from 1747 to 1764, wrote that not one single Black admitted by him to the Holy Communion had "turned out bad, or been in any scrape or disgrace to our Holy Profession."[35]

One of the Bishops of the Society for the Propagation of the Gospel in Foreign Parts suggested that Blacks should be

---

[35]Weatherford and Johnson, *Race Relations*, pp. 349-350.

trained to teach their own people. Therefore in 1741 two Blacks, Harry and Andrew, were purchased to be trained for this purpose. In 1744 they started a school in Charleston, South Carolina. Weatherford suggests that their pupils must have been free Blacks, since South Carolina in 1740 had passed a law prohibiting the teaching of slaves to read and write. This school was open until 1764.

Of the work done by religious sects during the Colonial period that of the Quakers was the most effective. One of the Quakers who took a prominent part in the education of Blacks was Anthony Benezet. In 1750 he established the first school for Blacks in Pennsylvania and taught there without charge. Through his influence the Society of Friends became interested in teaching the Blacks.

Negro Education and Revolutionary Leaders

During the latter part of the eighteenth century there was an increasing interest in the Blacks on the part of many of the leaders of the Revolution.

No one of the statesmen was more interested in the enlightenment of the Negro than Benjamin Franklin. He was made president of the Abolition Society of Philadelphia, which in 1774 founded a successful school for Negroes that was so well planned and maintained that it continued a hundred years.[36]

One of the outstanding Revolutionary leaders interested in the education of Blacks was a man who had come from Poland to fight in the cause of American freedom, General Kosciuszko. It was the intention of Kosciuszko to remain in the United States; but in March 1798 he was called home. On leaving he entrusted to Thomas Jefferson a will which shows his concern for the freedom and education of the Blacks:

I, Thaddeus Kosciuszko, being just on my departure from

[36]Carter G. Woodson, *The Education of the Negro Prior to 1861* (Washington, D. C.: The Association for the Study of the Negro Life and History, 1919), pp. 59-60.

America, do hereby declare and direct that should I make no other testamentary disposition of my property in the United States, I hereby authorize my friend, Thomas Jefferson, to employ the whole thereof in purchasing Negroes from among his own or others, and giving them liberty in my name; in giving them an education in trade or otherwise; in having them instructed for their new education in the duties of morality, which may make them good neighbors, good fathers and mothers, husbands and wives, in their duty as citizens; teaching them to be defenders of their liberty and country, of the good order of society, and in whatsoever may make them happy and useful.

5th of May 1798
T. Kosciuszko.

This will, written 65 years before the Emancipation Proclamation, showed Kosciuszko a pioneer in planning for freedom and education of the slaves. Unfortunately complications arose over the execution of the will and Kosciuszko's wishes were never carried out.

From the eighteenth century through the early part of the nineteenth little opposition to the instruction of the Negroes, slave or free, was seen. There was even a growing interest. Although South Carolina had made it unlawful to teach a slave and Georgia, in 1770, had passed a similar law, in all the other colonies education of the Blacks was encouraged, either by individuals, organizations, or the state itself. In 1788 New Jersey passed a law that made it compulsory for masters to give instruction to their slaves, "preliminary to emancipation." There were owners who took a personal interest in the education of their slaves, or of individual slaves, and gave them unusual opportunity. Such were the owners of Phillis Wheatley, a little girl bought in Boston in 1761, when she was but six years old. When the owners saw that she was eager to learn and showed aptitude for so doing, they gave her every encouragement possible. She became one of the outstanding figures of her day, the second woman poet to publish in America, her first published work appearing when she was only fourteen years old. Sometimes a master freed a slave who showed himself ambitious for an education, or allowed him to purchase himself, as was the case with James Derham, who was trained in medicine by each of his physician owners and finally allowed to buy his freedom and set up his own practice.

Various organizations, religious and secular, concerned themselves with the education of Blacks. The Presbyterian Synod of New York and Pennsylvania in 1787 urged its membership to give their slaves education to prepare them for a better enjoyment of freedom. The Quakers continued their interest in the enlightenment of the Black, establishing schools in Pennsylvania, Virginia, Maryland, and North Carolina. The Catholics were especially active in Maryland, but "wherever they had the opportunity to give the slaves religious instruction, they generally taught the unfortunates everything that would broaden their horizon and help them understand life."[37]

In order to prepare the Blacks for the freedom that during the latter part of the eighteenth century seemed inevitable and to take care of those already freed, abolition societies were established in various sections of the country. By 1791 twelve such societies were in existence. They took a leading part in the beginning of formal education for Blacks. The New York society, known as the Manumission Society, established in 1787 the first secular school for Blacks in New York, the African Free School. In 1834 there were seven of these African schools, which were taken over by the newly organized New York Public School Society.

Another factor was what was being done for and by the free Blacks, both in the South and in the North. For the most part the free Blacks were concentrated in the cities. In some cities they were helping to support the schools to which they sent their children. For instance, in Charleston, South Carolina, the Brown Fellowship Society as early as 1790 founded a school for Black children. In New Orleans there were schools supported largely by Blacks. In 1807 three former slaves built the first school for Blacks in Washington, D.C., and engaged a white teacher. Daniel Coker, a Negro Methodist missionary, had an academy in Baltimore before 1812. In Philadelphia the free people of color organized a society that in 1804 opened a school for Blacks. Of the sixteen schools for Blacks in that city

---

[37]Woodson, *The Education of the Negro Prior to 1861*, p. 108.

37

in 1822, eleven were taught by teachers of African descent. *The Newport* (Rhode Island) *Mercury* of March 26, 1808, carried an announcement of the opening of a school by the African Benevolent Society for all Blacks "inclined to attend."

The Industrial Revolution, which resulted in the enlarging and the impersonalizing of the "cotton kingdom," was indirectly responsible for a growing opposition to the education of the Black. Another cause was several slave insurrections that took place during the early part of the nineteenth century. The slave states, one after another, passed laws prohibiting the teaching of slaves, and even restricting the education of free Blacks.

Some education was carried on in spite of these laws. Schools for free Blacks existed in most of the southern cities, and the laws did not succeed in closing all of these. Certain individuals defied the laws and taught their slaves or other Blacks. Some schools were conducted clandestinely. One school in Savannah that had been taught openly until 1829 then went "underground," but continued until 1844. The Union army in 1864 found a school in that city that had been taught secretly by a Black woman for thirty years. Many secret schools existed in Virginia. Horace Mann Bond sums up the situation thus:

> Perhaps the strangest commentary on the education of Negroes in the ante-bellum South is to be found in the census figures for 1850. In spite of the fact that the laws of every Southern state proscribed the education of slaves, and that in several of these states the prohibition extended to free Negro children, Mississippi was the only state reporting no Negroes attending school in that year.[38]

During the period of reaction against the education of Blacks there was a movement to send the Blacks "back where they came from," and there was no objection to the teaching of those who planned to settle in Liberia. This teaching, however, was limited to individuals, for several attempts to open schools for

---

[38]*The Education of the Negro in the American Social Order* (New York: Prentice-Hall, Inc., 1934), p. 177.

this purpose failed. Some of the Blacks were even trained in the professions.

There were individual Blacks who acquired knowledge in ingenious ways through their own initiative. The great Frederick Douglass was one of them. A kind mistress had started to teach him to read, but was forced to stop when her husband learned of the lessons. Thereafter Frederick learned by his own efforts:

Soon he managed to get a Webster's spelling-book, which he always carried with him when he went on his errands. After this, every time he went out he made new friends until the very boys who at first pounced upon him at every corner, now began to help him with his spelling lessons. One day while he was on his way to the shipyard, and just after he had gotten a spelling lesson at the corner, it occurred to him that the boys might also help him to learn to write.

While he was in the shipyard, he watched the carpenters finish pieces of timber for the different sides of the ship and mark each piece. For instance, a piece for the starboard side was marked "S". He soon learned for what these letters stood and how to make them. When he went out on the next errand, he said to the boys, "You can't make as good an 'S' as I can make." Such a challenge had to be met. They all dropped down on their knees and began to contest by making letters on the pavement. Frederick watched closely and learned to make for the first time many other letters. He kept at it until he learned to make them all.[39]

Of course the opportunity was not great, for Blacks to obtain formal education was greater in the free states than in the South. As public schools were established Blacks were admitted on an equality with whites, or appropriations were made for separate schools for them. As early as 1822 there was a tax-supported school for Blacks in Philadelphia. There were

[39]Elizabeth Ross Haynes, *Unsung Heroes* (New York: DuBois and Dill, Publishers, 1921), pp. 23-24.

such schools in several places in New England by 1818—Boston, Salem, New Haven, and Portland. In New York the African Free Schools became public schools in 1834, and in 1858 were transferred to the Board of Education, just then formed. In some parts of Ohio the Blacks were in mixed schools; in other parts, in separate ones. There were states, like Wisconsin, Michigan, and Iowa, where no distinctions were made. Separate schools were not necessarily a result of anti-Black bias. In some states or cities Blacks asked for separate schools. In most of the northern states their constitutionality was eventually challenged, they were later made discretionary, and finally abolished.

II. HIGHER EDUCATION
PRIOR TO EMANCIPATION

Important for the educational advance of the Black was the establishment of institutions of higher learning: Avery College in Pennsylvania in 1849, Lincoln University in Pennsylvania in 1854, and Wilberforce in Ohio in 1856. The latter was controlled by Blacks. There was another college which played a part in this advance, Oberlin, founded in 1835. When Professor Asa Mahan of Lane Seminary was asked in 1835 to take the presidency, he accepted only on condition that Blacks should be admitted on an equality with others. By the time of the Civil War one third of the student body of this college was Black.

Prior to 1861 a number of Blacks had obtained college or university training, or had educated themselves to the extent of entering a profession or passing examinations. Among those of the eighteenth century were the preachers Lemuel Haynes, Josiah Bishop, John Gloucester and John Chavis, and the physician James Derham. The first Black to be graduated from an American college was John R. Russworm, who received a degree from Bowdoin College in 1826. Soon after this, other college graduates began to appear. John V. Degrasse and Thomas J. White obtained degrees in medicine in 1849—also from Bowdoin. James McCune Smith was a graduate of the University of Glasgow. In law there were the following: Robert Morris, admitted to the Boston bar in 1850; John M. Langston, graduate of Oberlin, admitted to the bar in 1847; and Garrison Draper of Dartmouth, who passed the Maryland bar in 1857. About this time there was a slave, Harrison Ellis, in Alabama, who educated himself in the classics. Upon examination it was found that he was a Latin, Greek and Hebrew scholar. The Presbyterian Church thereupon purchased his freedom and he went to Liberia.

The ministers of the early nineteenth century included Alexander Crummell, who had studied at Cambridge University, England; James W. C. Pennington, who had a degree from the University of Heidelberg; Henry Highland Garnett, who had studied at Oneida Institute, New York; and Samuel Ringgold Ward, well versed in theology and the classics.

Of the Blacks who acquired an education in the classics a number became educators. John Chavis had schools for white boys. James Pennington for several years was president of Avery College. There were three Blacks on the staff of New York Central College: C. C. Reason, Professor of "belles-lettres" and French; George Vashon, professor of classics (afterward president of Avery College); and William G. Allen, professor of Greek, German rhetoric, and "belles-lettres."

During the Civil War the Union army had opened schools for the Blacks who flocked across their lines. In the first years after the war most of the private schools and colleges that exist today for Blacks were established, with the help of the Freedmen's Bureau, northern philanthropy, and church boards. Public schools were started in all the southern states, by the Reconstruction governments.

> . . . At no time and place in America has there been exemplified so pathetic a faith in education as the lever of racial progress. Grown men studied their alphabet in the field, holding the "blue-back speller" with one hand while they guided the plow with the other. Mothers tramped scores of miles to town where they could place their children in school. Pine torches illumined the dirt-floored cabins where men, women, and children studied far into the night. . . .[40]

[40]Bond, *The Education of the Negro in the American Social Order*, p. 23.

Two of the larger schools started during the Reconstruction period gave to the world a new philosophy in education. Hampton Institute was founded in Hampton, Virginia, in 1868.

A departure from the traditional curriculum was made in the emphasis that was laid upon work with the hands, as part of the training to fit the students for the various activities in a normal community. Today this does not sound revolutionary, for we are accustomed to all kinds of vocational courses in our schools. Hampton was the pioneer in this field. At first the emphasis was on teacher-training, but training in other vocations was added so that the men and women who went out from the school could take the lead in homemaking and community service. Tuskegee Institute, Tuskegee, Alabama, founded in 1880, also emphasized practical education. These two schools have had a worldwide influence in turning schools to a more practical application of knowledge.

Just before the Civil War slave labor had constructed in Talladega, Alabama, a building designed as an academy for sons of the planters. The American Missionary Association took it over for one of their schools, and "one of the first graduates of the new institution was an artisan who ten years before had helped to lay the brick for the schoolhouse."[41]

Fisk University, Nashville, Tennessee, which is one of the leading liberal arts colleges, is famous for being the first Black school to acquaint the world with the Spirituals. Three of the schools founded in Atlanta—Atlanta University, Morehouse College and Spelman College—were consolidated a few years ago to form a university. The largest of the Black educational institutions, Howard University, Washington, D.C., was started as a school for Black and white, young and old, prepared or unprepared. When the Freedmen's Bureau could no longer give it financial aid, Congress made an appropriation to enable it to continue; and ever since Howard has been largely supported by the federal government. A few years after its founding it became a college for Negroes, and is now a university. Other important institutions of higher learning for Blacks are Wilberforce University, in Wilberforce, Ohio; Lincoln University, at Lincoln University, Pennsylvania; Dillard University, in New Orleans, Louisiana; Morgan College, in Baltimore,

---

[41]Embree, *Brown America*, p. 108.

Maryland; Clark University, in Atlanta, Georgia; the Atlanta School of Social Work in Atlanta; Wiley University, in Marshall, Texas; Johnson C. Smith, in Charlotte, North Carolina; Bennett College for Women in Greensboro, North Carolina; Livingston College, in Salisbury, North Carolina; Knoxville College, in Knoxville, Tennessee; St. Augustine's College and Shaw University, in Raleigh, North Carolina.

While the Reconstruction governments were in power in the southern states there were mixed schools. In Arkansas, Louisiana, Mississippi, Florida, and South Carolina, Blacks were even elected to the state superintendency of schools. But as the conservatives were returned to the control of the state governments, dual systems of schools replaced the mixed systems, usually, however, with the stipulation that there be no difference in the quality of equipment and teaching staff of the two systems.

In spite of possible good intentions on the part of some of the state governments there has not been enough money to maintain two systems adequately, and therefore the Black schools have suffered. By the beginning of the twentieth century the status of these schools was not much better than it was in 1875. An exhaustive survey of conditions published by the Phelps-Stokes Fund in 1917 disclosed glaring inadequacies and inequalities. For instance, in the whole South there were only 64 high schools for Blacks. Buildings were dilapidated, equipment meager or lacking, teachers poorly trained and poorly paid. With the help of public and private funds, reforms were begun on all grade levels. By 1932 the number of high schools for Blacks in the South had increased to 1200. However, 230 counties still lacked any high school for Blacks, and another 195 counties provided no four-year high school for Blacks.

The migration of Blacks to cities and especially to cities of the North, which began to be felt in 1918, resulted in greater educational opportunities for more members of the group. At the close of the Civil War it was estimated that 90 per cent of the Blacks were illiterate. By 1930 illiteracy had been reduced to 20 per cent, but in 1940 it was only 10 per cent.

III. THE BLACK PRESS: A SOCIAL INSTITUTION

With the end of the civil conflict, Black newspapers began appearing all over the country. In the South thirty-four newspapers edited by Blacks entered the journalistic field between 1865 and 1880. The majority of them, however, were published for only a short time. In the North and East combined, only eight Black newspapers were published. Outnumbering the North was the Middle West, with a record of fourteen journals. In the West there was only one, the *Elevator*.[1]

Black newspapers still were not published primarily for the purpose of making money. From the commercial point of view most of them were unprofitable. They were conceived with the definite purpose of raising the Black to a higher cultural level. They were regarded by Blacks much the same as were the school and the church—as social institutions.

From every available source the newspapers gathered facts and information pertaining to the new position of the Black. They made these facts intelligible to the unenlightened Blacks and to sympathizing whites. They attempted to weaken and possibly eliminate racial prejudice, to break down the barriers of ignorance and bigotry, and to support policies of political and economic betterment. The publishers were aware of these three tasks of their papers and were conscious of their responsibility. To them their papers were not primarily a matter of business.

Most of the newspapers of this period lacked large capital investments, were built upon a precarious economic basis, and could exist only by extreme sacrifices and dauntless energy of their contributors. However, one paper of this period, the *Louisianian*,[2] was on a firm financial basis. It derived a larger income from advertisements than did any of the other papers. Also, since it served as a mouthpiece of the national Republican party, it received as paid matter, official documents decreed by law to be published by the Louisiana State Legislature.

---

[1]This paper is not to be confused with the publication of the same name published in Albany, N. Y., 1841-1842 (see p. 37).

[2]Founded in New Orleans, LA., 1870.

Today the most important source of revenue for newspapers is advertisements. This did not hold true for the Black newspapers in the Reconstruction period. None of the Black papers except the *Louisianian* seemed to have derived from advertisements a profit worth mentioning. Out of a sample of ten newspapers analyzed, not a single one carried advertisements amounting to more than 12 per cent of its space, and five carried less than 4 per cent. The volume of advertisements in one of the papers was as little as ½ per cent. (See Table I.) The rates were not sufficiently high to make a small quantity profitable. The charge for space was based on what was called a square, which consisted of ten lines, or the space necessary for ten lines, of eight-point type. The rates varied with different newspapers from fifty cents to two dollars a square. Advertising rates were not set in accordance with any circulation ratio, and often papers did not adhere to their given rates. Instead, they charged the highest amount the advertiser was willing to pay. The Athens *Blade*, founded in 1879, exhibited no qualms about bargaining with the advertiser and stated: "Advertisements will be put in on the most liberal terms. Persons desiring to advertise can call or write for terms."[3] The majority of the advertisements were limited to one square, which allowed for no more than the name, address, and a short description of the business. The types of advertisements found in the papers examined (Table II) indicate that the income from this source would necessarily have been limited.

Another source of income of the newspapers was the sale to readers. Some of the Black newspapers were circulated over wide areas. The *Colored Tennessean* of Nashville, Tennessee, for instance, established in 1866 apparently as the second Black weekly in the South, had subscribers in most of the southern states and in several northern states, such as New Jersey, New York, and Ohio. Places where the paper was for sale are listed as follows: [4]

STATE OF TENNESSEE	STATE OF ALABAMA
Maysville	Athens

---

[3]Scattered issues.
[4]*The Colored Tennessean*, March 31, 1866.

Jonesboro	Hunterville
Unita	Florence
Greensville	Tuscumbia
Franklin	
Memphis	

STATE OF GEORGIA	STATE OF NEW YORK
Atlanta	New York City
Athens	STATE OF NEW JERSEY
Macon	Jersey City
Savannah	
STATE OF SOUTH CAROLINA	STATE OF KENTUCKY
Charleston	Bowling Green

Agents receiving the weekly at a given point covered nearby places, but sometimes there were as many as six representatives in one town. The number of subscribers to the *Elevator* was given as 800, according to a statement made by the publisher. However, the weekly journal was well received, and it was necessary for the editor to print two hundred additional copies after the printing of the first issue.[5]

For the sake of inducing merchants to advertise, the various newspapers invariably gave in grossly exaggerated figures the total number of copies printed weekly. Not even *Rowell's Newspaper Directory* gave circulation figures that were altogether reliable, since they had no way of checking. According to Rowell, Bowley's Georgetown *Planet*, founded in 1873, had an estimated circulation of 280, while the *Missionary Record* had an estimated circulation of 720 to 1000.[6] The Huntsville *Gazette*, founded in 1873 in Huntsville, Alabama, claimed that

... The Gazette lives because it is a necessity. The peculiar state of affairs which called it into existence mapped out its course. In Alabama it has become a household word in nearly

---

[5]*The Elevator*, May 5, 1865.
[6]*Rowell's Newspaper Directory*, 1873, p. 200.

every colored family, finding its way to friends visited by no other journal.[7]

TABLE I
ANALYSIS OF TEN NEWSPAPERS
SHOWING RATIO OF ADVERTISING SPACE
TO SPACE DEVOTED TO NEWS EDITORIALS

Percent of Advertising Space Number of Issues	to News and Editorial Space
1	.5%
1	1.0%
1	2.6%
2	3.3%
2	4.0%
2	8.0%
1	9.1%
1	9.5%
2	10.0%
1	12.0%

Analysis of these data shows that there were five newspapers in which the percentage of advertising space was 4 or less and five in which it was 4.1 up to 12. Practice with regard to the amount of space devoted to advertisements had not begun to take on any uniform character.

The *South Carolina Leader*, which was founded in 1865 and published in Charleston, claimed for a year that it was the only Republican paper printed in South Carolina. After the circulation of this paper had reached North Carolina, Georgia, and Florida, the publisher attempted to extend it further by offering premiums according to the number of subscriptions solicited. This seems to have been the first subscription campaign sponsored by a Black journal. The premiums offered included the following items: [8]

120 Subscriptions	1 Horace Water's Organ	Value	$150
100 "	1 " " Melodeon	"	115
75 "	1 Leavitt's Sewing Machine	"	90

---

[7]Huntsville *Gazette*, June 1881.
[8]*The South Carolina Leader*, October 14, 21, 1865.

TABLE II
TYPES OF ADVERTISEMENTS IN NEWSPAPERS
1860–1880

B

Bakery
Barbershop
Billiard and Pool
Blacksmith
Boats
Book Concern

C

Carpenters
Churches
City Hack
Clothing Stores
Coal
Coffins
Cooking Grease

D

Dentist
Dressmaker
Druggist
Dry Goods
Dyers

F

Fraternal
  organizations and
  Emblems
Furniture Stores
Furs

G

Grocery Stores
Gold Watches
Guns and Pistols

H

Hairdresser
Hair Preparation
Harness
Hatter
Help Wanted
House Painting and
  Graining

I

Ice Cream
Insurance
Iron Works

M

Mattresses
Millinery
Music Teacher

O

Organ and musical
  Instruments

P

Patent Medicine
Physicians
Piano
Picture Frame
Plumber
Political
  Announcements
Prospectus of
  Newspapers and
  Magazines

R

Railroad
Rest and Boarding
  House
Restaurants

S

Savings Bank
School
Sewing Machines
Show Factory
Situation Wanted

T

Tailor

U

Undertaker

W

Wash Blue
Wines and Liquors

45	"	Set of Chamber Furniture	"	65
35	"	Sewing Machine	"	40
20	"	Railway Timekeeper	"	25
15	"	Bible	"	20
10	"	Horace Greeley's Album	"	10
5	"	Family Gem Sewing Machine	"	5
1	"	Abe Lincoln's Photo		

At the time the subscription campaign was being conducted, the *South Carolina Leader* claimed that it had "the largest circulation of any weekly in the Southern States."

The subscription rates of the newspapers also varied with the individual papers. Ordinarily a single copy was sold for five cents, but some papers were double that amount. Yearly subscriptions were offered at a reduced price. As a special courtesy, ministers and teachers were given a still lower rate by some of the newspapers. The rates by mail for individual subscriptions varied from five cents to ten cents for a single copy.

Ladies' quilting circles and church groups could subscribe at a club rate. The annual rates of the *Colored Tennessean*, for example, ran as follows: [9]

Club of five to one address	$ 6.25
Club of ten to one address	12.00
Club of twenty to one address	20.00

The subscriptions, bulk sales, and advertisements meant very little in the total financial operation of most of the Black journals. The exceptions could be counted on one hand.

Most of the papers needed additional financial aid. Some of them appealed to their members for support necessary to make the papers permanent institutions,[10] as did the *Colored Citizen* of Cincinnati, Ohio, founded in 1863 and published by an association of colored men, despite the fact that it had the advantage of owning a printing shop that supplied a reserve fund.

However, weeklies that owned their printing plants usually

---

[9] *The Colored Tennessean*, scattered issues, 1877.
[10] *The Colored Citizen*, May 19, 1866.

were able to maintain themselves. Newspapers that owned their plants, according to their advertisements, included the *National Era*, the *Missionary Record*, the Athens *Blade*, the *Louisianian*, the *Colored American*, founded in 1865 and published in Augusta, Ga.; Charleston *Journal*, founded in 1866; *People's Advocate*, founded and published in Washington, D.C., in 1876; and the *Tribune* of New Orleans, a daily, founded in 1864.

Once the publishers possessed a few cases of type and a printing press, they could calculate on the frequency of publication. Paper stock for printing the journals could be secured gratuitously from the Baltimore Newspaper Union. On two pages of a broadside the newspaper union printed patent medicine advertisements with some reading material; and the reverse side of each was available for original matter.[11] Advertisers were cut off from their supplies when the war started. Naturally they were crippled. Some of them even had to print their newspaper on wallpaper.[12] Among the Black newspapers of the Reconstruction period, the *Missionary Record* possibly made the poorest showing in mechanical makeup—the workmanship in its printing plant was of low quality.[13]

However, the task ahead of the Black newspapers was more important to them than were financial gains; and also more important than the mechanical makeup. What inspired the Black newspapers of this period was responsibility for the advancement of the Black man's cause. This is reflected in the declarations and slogans printed on the mastheads of the Black papers. Some of these declarations and slogans were voluble. For example, the *National Era* printed this declaration in every issue:

> . . . The National Era will partake of a twofold nature—that of an Advocate and Educator. As an Advocate it will assert and maintain every right pertaining to the American citizen, independent of race, color, or accident of birth. It will demand

---

[11]In computing figures for Table I, only advertisements yielding an income to the paper were included.

[12]James Melvin Lee, *History of Journalism*, p. 285.

[13]*The Missionary Record*, August 26, 1871.

the recognition of these rights wherever the Constitution extends or the national insignia waves. As an Educator, its columns will be a special medium for the effective diffusion of right principles as much needed instructions, and for the inclusion of those habits of industry and self-reliance conducive to independent manhood, and give vitality and energy to free government, insuring in return blessings to the governed.[14]

Slogans of a few of the other Black papers are listed in Table III.

The readers seemed to have an appreciation for the efforts being made by the Black newspapers in the work for the advancement of Blacks. The esteem in which some of their readers held these papers may be seen in a letter[15] appearing in an issue of the *Elevator*, which reads in part:

. . . Your valuable paper, as its name indicates, "a journal of progress", has not been received as regularly as desired, but always welcome. You will please accept my grateful acknowledgments for occasional copies of journals like the *People's Journal, The Communicator, The Right Way, The Flag,* and others devoted to the cause which greatly interests us all. In this far upper country such papers are a feast, which I assure you are duly appreciated and the donors gratefully remembered.

Napoleon III not long ago said, "If there are men who do not comprehend their epoch, I am not one of their number." It was much to say, but his success has justified it. In the great pending crisis, affecting the whole race of colored men, we want men who comprehend their epoch—who have the ability, courage and desire to favor the cause of progress. To this end let the school house arise in every hamlet, free to all, of every caste or color. Churches will follow and journals

---

[14]*The National Era*, August 14, 1873.
[15]Sent to the *Elevator* by a reader from an Indian territory in the far west.

spring up and disseminate intelligence to our hitherto enslaved but now free and progressive race. And let all remember that "He who would be free must himself strike the blow."

During the period 1860 to 1880, Black newspapers made no attempt to keep in step with journalism of the period. White newspapers followed Charles Dana of the New York *Sun*, in 1860, and put an end to personal journalism. The front rank of editors who followed this impersonal approach were Edwin Lawrence Godkin, editor of the *Evening Post* and the *Nation*; Henry Raymond, editor of the *New York Times*; and James Bennett, editor of the New York *Herald*. Godkin became a pivot of liberal, intelligent thinking in this period.

Competition in the business of gathering and disseminating news grew by leaps and bounds. Taking advantage of the temperament of the public, Horace Greeley had even initiated the practice of selling dailies for one cent.[16]

Certainly, if Black journals had not been subsidized by philanthropists who were interested in the social adjustment of the Black, many would have expired within a short time after their first publication.

The average weekly newspaper consisted of four pages, with a depth of twenty inches, and were divided into four thirteen-em columns. Roughly the column width was two and one-fourth inches. Successful publications like the *People's Advocate* fell into this class. More ambitious undertakings, such as the *Louisianian*, appeared in eight pages with seven columns. Frequently, however, the latter dwindled down to four pages. There were no sensational headings or large-size type used to head a news story. A single line in capital letters of eight- or ten-point type indicated the subject matter of the article. Until 1867, the size type used for headlines to caption articles was of the same size as the body of the story. Apparently the first use of large headline type appeared in the April 10, 1987 issue of the *Loyal Georgian*,[17] when the newspaper complained of a "Brutal and Cowardly Outrage."

---

[16]George Payne, *History of Journalism*, pp. 153-163.

[17]This paper was founded in 1866 and is not the same as the *Loyal Weekly Georgian*.

TABLE III
SLOGANS OF BLACK NEWSPAPERS
IN RECONSTRUCTION PERIOD

The Weekly Anglo-African	"Man must be Free, if not Through Law, Why then Above Law."
The Southern Workman	"Devoted to the Industrial Classes of the South."
The South Carolina Leader	"First the Head, Then the Ear, After the Full Corn in the Ear"—Paul.
The Missionary Record	"Remember that ye Were Strangers Ready to Die."
Huntsville *Gazette*	"With Charity for All, and Malice Toward None."
The Colored Tennessean	"With Malice Toward None, With Charity for All."
The Loyal Georgian	"Taxation Without Representation is Tyranny."
The Elevator	"Equality Before the Law."
The Colored Citizen (Cincinnati)	"Nothing that Concerns Mankind is Foreign to Me."
Charleston *Journal*	"Thou Shalt Love they Neighbor as Thyself."
Athens *Blade*	"The Arm of Justice Cannot—Will Not Sleep."
The American Citizen	"Africa's Friends our Friends; Her Enemies our Enemies."
The People's Advocate	"Principles, not Men; but Men as Representatives of Principles."

The poor mechanical equipment of the Black newspapers accounted for their poor appearance. Some of the Black newspapers, however, looked better than the southern papers published by the whites during the war period. The white southern papers, being dependent upon the North for machines, paper stock, and foundry type materials, the journalist opportunities lay in his ability to influence the public by his own opinion. In an editorial in the New York *Tribune*, early in 1868, he declared:

... An essential element in the truly literary or scholarly character is a love of truth for truth's sake. Nothing but this passion for the dissemination of sound and true views can compensate the editor for his interest and unremitting labor.

He who is not conscious of having first interpreted events, suggested policies, corrected longstanding errors, or thrown forward a more searching light in the path of progress, has never tasted the luxury of journalism. It is the province of journalism to lead and to lead.[18]

The Black press tried to imitate Greeley's style of personal journalism and his editorial policy. Of course, they could not attain the unique style, typical of articles in the columns of the *Tribune*; but all of them caught his vision. The imitation of Greeley accounted for the appearance of news colored with opinion instead of the cold presentation of events. The Black press still adhered to a personal journalism primed "to lead and to lead" a bewildered, frightened mass of Blacks to the tune of social change caused by the decay of the cotton culture of the South.

There was a difference in purpose, content, and interpretation between the Black newspapers and the weekly and daily papers published for the benefit of foreigners who came to the United States during this period. The foreign language papers, printed in the native language of its readers, acted as a temporary guide to the newcomers while they were seeking employment, learning something of the English language, and adjusting themselves to a new environment. These papers printed articles telling "the story of American business, pluck, enterprise, and achievement in discovering and mining the treasures of the earth, in manufacturing, in trade, in literature, in science and invention, and in art."[19] They also carried a large volume of news of social and political happenings in the native lands of their various readers. This situation resulted from the fact that many of the immigrants had not lost consciousness

---

[18]G. W. Bleyer, *Main Currents in the History of Journalism* (Boston: Houghton Mifflin Co., 1913), p. 233.

[19]American Association of Foreign Language Newspapers, New York *Tribune*, June 30, 1919 (page advertisement).

of their nationality. Likewise, they seem to have been more concerned about international than national affairs. Moreover, the papers were not always accurate interpreters of American life because of the inability of some editors to read English.[20] Some of the editors of the foreign language newspapers were well versed in German and on coming to the United States they translated information for their readers from German sources. This meant that they saw America through another foreigner's eyes.

The Black newspapers, on the other hand, were then, as they are now, a part of our American culture and were concerned about important national political and social issues, especially as they pertained to the Blacks.

The primary source of general news for the Black newspapers was clippings from white northern dailies. From the credit lines of many articles, it is evident that innumerable items reprinted from a large daily had been copied three or four times before they had reached the columns of a particular Black newspaper. In fact, until very recently, a host of weeklies relied upon the daily press for general news. Replying to an attack on big dailies playing up crimes committed by Blacks, Victor Lawson, late publisher of the *Chicago Daily News*, told an assembly of Black editors convening in Chicago in 1927 that if it were not for this practice, Black papers would perish.

Other material printed in the Black papers during Reconstruction came from government bulletins, records of court proceedings, church programs, and contributions by readers. The newspapers were conscious of the inadequate knowledge of the mass of Blacks who were cultivating land without an overseer. As slaves, they had been accustomed to judging their crops to a large extent by natural phenomena and following the instructions of the plantation master. As freedmen, they had to rely upon their own abilities, and the newspapers endeavored to aid them by circulating agricultural hints issued by the federal government. This information was important because the chief

[20]Thomas Capek, *The Czechs in America* (Boston: Houghton Mifflin Company, 1920), p. 144.

occupation of Blacks was farming. Decisions of local and federal courts were also important because they took on the significance of the laws. Similar interest was given to Congressional resolutions bearing on the status of the Black. These documents were printed at length. The newspaper publishers commented freely on resolutions of this sort and advised their readers as to what action they should take when such action was expedient.

The church was another source of news. Besides being a place for religious services, the church was a center for community events. Concerts, spelling bees, and entertainments were given there. These affairs, which brought many Blacks together and were significant outlets for their emotions, also furnished news items. Then, too, the editor received many letters giving complete accounts of civic activities within the community and in nearby communities. There were persons who desired to inform their neighbors of their ill luck or good fortune. Such items as these found space in personal columns. Likewise, space was given to writers of poetry. Other types of material printed in these papers are indicated in Table IV. Sources of the matter have already been suggested in some instances, but a complete listing may be found in Table V.

In spite of limited sources for material, the Black press was a social institution in that it created a "phase of the public mind, not different in its ultimate nature from public opinion, though often seeming, on account of its permanence and the visible customs and symbols in which it is clothed, to have a somewhat distinct and independent existence."[21]

IV. BLACK EDITORS

The editor of a Black newspaper was generally also the owner. He carried on his duties as editor usually in conjunction with another vocation, this dual function serving two useful purposes. First, it gave him economic security; and second, it

---

[21]Charles H. Cooley, *Social Organization* (New York: Charles Scribner's Sons, 1911), p. 313.

TABLE IV
TYPE OF MATERIAL PRINTED IN BLACK NEWSPAPERS

Government	Church	Editorial	Miscellaneous
Agricultural hints to farmers	Community Events	Letters to editor	Personals
Court proceedings	Sermons	News Items	Poetry
State legislation	Obituaries	Special articles	
Congressional resolutions			

TABLE V
SOURCE OF MATERIAL IN BLACK NEWSPAPERS

Contributors	Exchange	Exchange	Government
Editor	Readers	Reprints from Black newspapers	Courts
Reporter	Ministers		State Records
	Editor's personal correspondence	Clippings from white newspapers	Federal bulletins
Editorial opinion			

gave him immediate access to sources of practical information. Circumstances surrounding the birth and upbringing of the editors varied widely, but it is possible to examine and make a general classification of some types of Black editors (Table VI).

For instance, Frederick Douglass was an illustrious example of a runaway slave who rose to be a leader of his people. He was born in 1817 on the eastern shore of Maryland. From recollections of his early childhood, he has given a narrative of starvation, of sharing meat bones with dogs, of hard work, and of the cracking of cowhide whips over his mother's back. Frederick was sent as a house servant to a Baltimore family shortly after he had reached his tenth birthday. Through his charm and manners, he won the interest of his new mistress, and over her husband's protest, she taught Frederick to read and write. To Frederick, this enlightenment meant liberation and the beginning of a new life. When he was a young man he

57

ran away to New Bedford. There by day he sawed wood, dug cellars, and shoveled coal to gain a livelihood. By night he continued to study, for he dreamed that something better was in store for him. Something was, for he achieved distinction as a lecturer and became the successful editor of a newspaper.

Unlike Douglass, many of the editors who were born in slavery but who acquired knowledge of the alphabet were preachers. In some of the Black churches, as recently as the early part of 1920, it was not uncommon for some Blacks, weary of unskilled labor, to answer "the call" to preach. A "sudden call" to preach was not infrequently a part of the careers of newspaper editors during the Reconstruction period. These "calls," supposedly word from God, had a mystic aspect, but also often a very realistic one; it was one way the Black had of improving his status with impunity. Whites interfered rarely when a Black received the "call to preach." Although the religious beliefs of the whites were warped by political traditions, the whites were, for religious reasons, reluctant to interfere with Black preachers. They were in fear of disregarding the dictates of God. Consequently, the easiest way out for the Black who had learned his ABC's and who desired to escape bondage was to answer "the call." While carrying on in the ministry, these "decreed disciples of God" set about to improve their social status. Often the next move was to enter the newspaper field.

Not all of the preachers were as distinguished as Richard Harvey Cain, who carried the Bible in one hand and his newspaper in the other, and became a leader of his people. Cain was born in 1825 in the "Old Dominion"; his parents found their way to Ohio during his early childhood. In his youth he worked as a steamboat hand on a canal boat. Around 1844 he turned from unskilled labor and took up preaching under the jurisdiction of the Methodist Episcopal Church. Later, realizing his limitations because of his lack of academic training, he entered Wilberforce University. The school, which was supported by the African Methodist Episcopal Church, trained him for service in their denomination. Appointed as minister in one of their churches in Charleston, S. C., he became active in local affairs. Charleston in 1865 rivaled only New Orleans, La., in political folly as a result of ignorance of the Blacks and bargaining for votes and jobs, ballot-box stuffing, and other corrupt practices. This city was the stronghold for the Republican

TABLE VI
OCCUPATIONS OF BLACK EDITORS: 1860-1880

NAME	OCCUPATION
Adams, E. J.	Chaplain-Agent of Educational Department of Freedom's Bureau
Allen, William G.	Unknown
Bowley, James A.	Showman
Bell, Philip A.	Unknown
Brooks, R. R.	Minister
Brown, J. M.	Minister
Bryant, John	Soldier
Cain, Richard	Bishop—Congressman—President of College
Campbell, Jabez	Minister
Cromwell, John	Lawyer
Cromwell, R. I.	Physician
Day, W. H.	Minister—Teacher
DeLaney, Martin	Physician—Army Major
Daney, John C.	Minister
Douglass, Lewis	Practical printer
Dupee, George W.	Unknown
Freeman, John J.	Unknown
Garnett, Henry Highland	Minister—U. S. Minister to Liberia
Green, R. A.	Physician
Grenner, Richard T.	Teacher
Gibbs, Mifflin W.	Government service
Hamilton, Robert	Practical printer
Hamilton, Thomas	Bookkeeper
Heard, W. H.	Minister
Hodges, Willis	Practical printer
Jones, A. C.	Court stenographer
Lynch, John R.	Congressman
Martin, John Sella	Minister
Mayers, Stephen	Practical printer
Murray, W. H.	Teacher
Perry, Rufus L.	Minister—Teacher
Peters, P. B.	Unknown
Pinchback, P. B. S.	Soldier—Lieutenant-Governor of Louisiana

Pledger, W. A.	Unknown
Randolph, B. F.	Army Chaplain—Politician
Ray, Charles B.	Minister
Rush, R. O.	Unknown
Sampson, John P.	Minister
Shuften, John T.	U. S. Commissioner
Simmons, Wm. S.	Minister—President Negro State University of Kentucky
Smalls, Robert	State Senator
Spellman, James J.	Special U. S. Lumber Agent
Steward, O. M.	Practical printer
Tanner, Benjamin T.	Minister
Trevigne, Paul	Teacher
Ward, Samuel	Minister
Whipper, W. J.	Lawyer—Politician
White, W. J.	Unknown
Williams, Daniel	Physician
Woolfork, P. H.	Practical printer
Zuille, John J.	Practical printer

party. About 90 per cent of the Republican voters were Blacks; and, as a means of reaching this big group, the *South Carolina Leader* was started by T. Hurley and Company. Allen Coffin, a proud Yankee, was its editor for a time, but he soon grew dissatisfied with the salary the company paid and resigned.[1] Cain became his successor. Associated with him was another Black, Alonzo Ranzier. In the spring of 1867, Ranzier was replaced as associate editor of Robert Elliot, who later became a representative in Congress. Out of his zeal for the advancement of the Black, Cain organized a stock company, whose shares were held by Blacks, to take over the ownership of the *South Carolina Leader*.[2] Cain was not scholarly in his writings but managed through morals drawn from Biblical parables to

---

[1]Robert H. Woody, *Republican Newspapers of South Carolina*, Virginia Historical Association, p. 15.

[2]*Ibid.*, pp. 15-16. Under the new management, April 7, 1868, the paper's name was changed to the *Missionary Record*.

reach the minds of the Blacks. Besides attaining political success, advancing from the State Senate to the House of Representatives in Congress, he was elected to the highest position in his church, the bishopric.

Quite different from the other editors mentioned, Benjamin Tucker Tanner had had some educational advantages at an early age. His parents were free Blacks in Pennsylvania, where he was born on December 25, 1820. He studied at Avery College in Allegheny City, Pennsylvania, for five years. Because of his father's death, he was forced to support himself and his mother by barbering while in college. His college training was supplemented by a three-year course in Western Theological Seminary. At the age of twenty-five, Tanner received his first appointment, in the Methodist Church in Washington, D. C. About two years later the Freedmen's Society secured his services to assist in organizing a common school. In 1856, the church convention elected him editor of the *Christian Recorder*. He held this position for sixteen years. On his death, one of the editorial comments written of him said:

. . . He was risen from a successful barber to be the king of Negro editors. His pen is sharper than his razor, and his editorial chair is finer than the barber chair. The church and race will long remember Dr. B. T. Tanner for the part he has taken in reconstruction of the South, for his words of encouragement.[3]

Successful as a minister and later engaged as newspaper editor was John Sella Martin. He was born September 27, 1832 in Charlotte, North Carolina. John knew only his mother, who was a slave. When he was six years old, his mother and sister were sold to a family in Columbus, Georgia. Later he himself was sold to an old wealthy bachelor to become his valet, and traveled with him throughout the country. As his master began having difficulty with his eyesight, he instructed John to perform secretarial duties. When John was eighteen years old, his

---

[3]W. S. Simmons, *Men of Mark* (Cleveland: G. M. Revell and Co., 1887), p. 988.

master died, and by his will gave freedom to his servant. Through a scheme of whites, however, in Mobile, Alabama, John was sold back into slavery in 1852, and was sent to New Orleans, Louisiana. Three years later he escaped on a steamer and eventually arrived safely in Chicago. Soon after, he went to Detroit, where he studied under the tutelage of an able Baptist minister. After his ordination as a minister in Buffalo, New York, in 1859, he took up the serious study of writing prose and poetry. His ability as a writer and speaker gained him considerable attention. Within two years, he was given the opportunity to visit in England for six months. On his return to America, he worked as co-editor of the *National Era* and later became the editor of the *Louisiana*.[4]

Mention should be made of two other ministers, B. F. Randolph and E. J. Adams, editors of the Charleston *Journal*. Their personal histories are unknown. Whereas Randolph was primarily interested in politics, his associate devoted his attention mainly to a religious program. The publisher claimed that the Charleston *Journal* was the best family paper printed in the interest of colored people in the South.[5] Because of his aggressive leadership, Randolph was murdered in Charleston on October 5, 1868.

The life stories of some other newspaper editors are strikingly different from the careers of men we have mentioned so far. R.C.O. Benjamin landed in America by accident. He was born on the island of St. Keys, British West Indies, March 31, 1855. At an early age he was sent to England to study under a private tutor in preparation for college. After three years in Trinity College, the spirit of adventure lured him to the sea. When the ship on which he was working docked in New York City, Benjamin decided to give up the sea. One of his first jobs was with the New York *Star* as soliciting agent and office clerk. Upon making the acquaintance of J. J. Freeman, editor of the *Progressive American*, he was made city editor of that journal. In 1876 Benjamin became a naturalized citizen. At different times, he owned and edited several newspapers, including the

---

[4]Brown, *The Rising Sun*, p. 536.
[5]Charleston *Journal*, October 4, 1866.

Colored Citizen (Pittsburgh, Pennsylvania), the *Chronicle* (Evansville, Indiana), and the *Negro American* (Birmingham, Alabama).[6]

Nothing of romance, color, and the splendor surrounding a character in fiction is missing in the life of Binkney Stewart Pinchback, "the gentleman from Louisiana," editor and publisher of the *Louisianian*. From cabin boy on a canal boat, he rose to the elective office of lieutenant-governor of Louisiana, frequently being called upon to serve temporarily as governor. Pinchback can be pictured in a political setting similar to that in which Huey Long was found almost sixty years later. Born on a Mississippi plantation, of slave mother and white planter father, Pinchback enjoyed liberty from the cradle. His family lost its economic security when "the big man," as the Black family called the planter, died. Two years of high school training received in Cincinnati concluded his formal education.[7] The political controversies in which he was involved caused ignoble aspersions to be cast on him. Through his medium, the *Louisianian*, he contended that his political efforts were motivated by a desire to serve his people.

Some men who were trained for professions later entered the journalistic field. Their professional training indicated that they were of free birth. Many of them published their own sheets. To this group belong Philip H. Murray, who taught school and published the St. Louis *Advocate*; George W. Williams, who was trained in a theological seminary and was encouraged by Horace Greeley to write; Martin Delaney, a medical doctor, who served in the United States Army; R. I. Cromwell, a physician practicing in New Orleans; John W. Cromwell, who won distinction as a lawyer; and John T. Shuften, United States Commissioner stationed at Atlanta, Georgia.

Paul Trevigne, who was born of Creole parents in 1825 at New Orleans, was another editor who had been trained for a profession. He received a well-planned education in preparation for teaching, the vocation he followed for forty years.[8] As

[6]Simmons, *Then of Mark*, p. 991.

[7]*Ibid.*, p. 759.

[8]Rodolphe L. Desdunes, *Nos Hommes et Notre Histoire* (Montreal: Arbour & Dupont, 1911), p. 90.

the leader of a small group, he became editor of *L'Union*, founded in 1862. Two pages of the paper were printed in French for the benefit of the Creole population and the other two in English. In the French section there were literary contributions from France, England, and Spain. Trevigne was especially interested in politics.

Practical printing was another starting point for the careers of Black editors in the Reconstruction period. Printers who had been trained in the offices of daily papers possessed, for that reason, a skill in which the other editors and publishers were deficient. Seven of the fifty-one editors listed in Table VI belong to this group. Stephen Mayers was one of them. He was born a slave in Rensselaer County, New York, but was freed before the Emancipation. His education was limited. However, his wife, Harriet Johnson, who had some ability in writing, aided her husband in the preparation of his newspaper copy.[9]

William Howard Day was another editor who was also a printer. He was born of free parents in New York City. He first attended the Folsona School, better known as Public School Number Two. He prepared for college at Northampton, Mass. There he learned the art of printing. In 1843, he entered Oberlin College at Oberlin, Ohio, and was graduated in 1847. William worked his way through school partly by employment in printing shops.[10] After his college education was finished, he moved to Cleveland, and in 1852 he was designated as chairman of the Committee of Citizens to greet Louis Kossuth of Hungary. This same year he established the *Aliened American*. Prior to this adventure he had worked as a compositor in the office of the Cleveland *True Democrat*, a white daily published by Thomas Brown and John C. Vaughn, former South Carolina slaveholders. Because of broken health, Day left Ohio and went to Canada. Later he traveled through England, Ireland, and Scotland, soliciting funds to erect schools for fugitives in the United States. Again he became active in the newspaper field, in 1870, taking over the editorship of *Our National Progress* of Wilmington, Delaware.[11]

---

[9]Garland Penn, *Afro-American Press*, p. 49.

[10]Simmons, *Men of Mark*, p. 988.

[11]*Ibid.*, p. 983. No issues of *Our National Progress* could be located.

The educated Blacks, from whom came the editors, were put in a position of trust. All of them had to work hard. They did not sit behind a desk, shouting out to reporters to cover assignments, but trudged about from place to place seeking information to improve the Blacks' condition. They were the symbol of a race. In short, they were leaders in their communities.

V. SOCIAL ADJUSTMENT OF BLACKS
(Government Control)

At the beginning of the Reconstruction period the caste system was replacing slavery as a means of preserving some of the traditions of the old social order. Particularly those whites who had been at the bottom of the class structure were interested in setting up caste barriers in order to bar social interaction between the races on the basis of freedom and equality. It is natural that a profound social change would call for government control to reduce and possibly eliminate violent resistance to that change. That control, as exerted by the government, we call enforcement of law. The government began to function as a regulator of individual behavior in interracial relations at the outbreak of the war, at first solely through the army, later chiefly through the Freedman's Bureau. The Black press felt that such a government function was necessary until both Blacks and whites had adjusted themselves to the new social alignment. The law enacting emancipation gave the Blacks a new social status, but the press regarded this proclamation as useless without an enforcement and regulative agency. Of course, a perfect democracy would not need such an agency; but where change disrupts basic mores of the social order, measures have to be taken to absorb the resultant shock to the traditional superiority of the dominant social group.

Congress had created the Freedman's Bureau by the Act of March 3, 1865, for the purpose of furthering racial adjustment. The bureau had its many faults in organization, for it was hurriedly established and it was dominated by the will of the army. The army officers selected to supervise the bureau were also placed in charge of local garrisons. In many instances they lost sight of the fact that the war was fought to preserve the Union, and treated the southern whites as despised aliens. Matters normally left to the civil branches of the government were taken over by the Bureau when the Black was involved. The army officers showed bias in favor of Blacks and discriminated against southern whites. The civilian staff of the bureau did very little to alleviate the condition, for among its personnel were cheats, thieves, and narrow-minded individuals.

Despite this condition, the newspapers endeavored to enlighten their readers on the necessity of having the government intervene during the transition to a new order. It was understood by the press that whatever rights were established by law had to be secured by a governmental agency.

Although the Freedman's Bureau was a part of Lincoln's Reconstruction plan, his assassination made the project's future a matter of doubt. The Blacks felt his passing as a personal loss, for the Civil War to them was waged for their freedom, and they had been effectively told to see in Lincoln their saviour. They feared that his successor, President Andrew Johnson, might not carry out the policies that Lincoln had followed. Their reactions are portrayed in the following news article:

> After the war the attitudes of whites in the South were divided along three distinct lines. The majority of the southern whites felt that it was expedient to yield, after the national government had stationed soldiers in their communities. A small group was willing to accept the social change, even without the persuasion of the federal troops. Another small group remained incorrigible and hoped eventually for the revival of the Southern Confederacy.[1]

In spite of these specific attitudes, the multitude of people had no precise opinion and thus were highly vulnerable to any suggestion they could comprehend. Therefore, the Black press felt that the government, in the interests of both the Blacks

---

[1]Carl Schurz, *The New South* (New York: American News Co., 1885), p. 1-32.

and the redefined democracy, should strengthen the progressive attitudes. Especially, the *Elevator* stated emphatically that the government had to set up an agency to aid the Black to advance to a new status.[2] Observations from different localities made it clear that a regulative agency was imperative in order to meet the difficulties of a complex situation that included the adjustment of Blacks as hired laborers, the prey of carpetbaggers on the ignorant masses, and corrupt practices in political affairs. In Mississippi and South Carolina laws were passed to supercede Reconstruction legislation. For instance, laws were enacted making it illegal for railroad employees to sell Blacks first-class passage on trains running through these states. The law became inactive only when Blacks traveled as attendants to whites. Other southern states either by political measures or devices that took advantage of the ignorance of Blacks also prevented the two races from mingling freely.[3]

. . . The tidings of the assassination of President Lincoln fell with grievous force upon the Blacks in the rebellious states. A letter from Vicksburg thus describes the effect of the news upon the colored people of that city:
—"The colored people, however, are the most demonstrative. A portrait of Mr. Lincoln was placed in front of a store, and has been continually surrounded by a crowd of them, each sorrowful, and many gazing with tearful eyes upon the shadow of him who is their redeemer, leading them out of gloom into the light of liberty. I stood for some time watching them—certainly one of the more intelligent, seeing I was a Yankee, commenced questioning me, and seemed afraid that Mr. Johnson, being a Southerner, would make some other arrangements, but were evidently much relieved by my assurance that the same justice would be meted out by him as under the old regime."[4]

---

[2]*The Elevator*, May 5, 1865.
[3]Ellis P. Oberholtzer, *History of the United States Since the Civil War* (New York: Macmillan Co., 1917), pp: 128-130.
[4]Editorial: "Andy Johnson and the Black Race," New York *Tribune* (Monday, May 8, 1865), Vol. XXXV, No. 7515.

It was not long before the Black newspapers became inquisitive about the acts of President Johnson. His public pledge in a speech to the Blacks at Nashville, Tennessee, the previous winter, to do everything in his power to secure them rights and justice, faded from their memories. As long as he had been vice president, there was little opportunity to judge Johnson's attitude, for he had been buoyed up and dominated by the spirit of his chief. When he became president, he soon revealed that he was dominated by the traditions emanating from his native Tennessee. The Black weeklies began searching for information that would show the direction in which the president was moving. A much-sought-after source of information about the conduct of the president was Brigadier General Fiske, who was considered an interested and benevolent friend to Blacks. Since Fiske had been placed in charge of the State of Tennessee, he had addressed throngs of Blacks and openly expressed joy over their freedom, assuring them God intended them to be free. This assurance of God's intention was contrary to the words of God coming from the mouths of preachers still under the influence of slavery. Now the mission of white political representatives of the government was to prove that there was a resemblance between Blacks and whites. General Fiske put the Black man in the jury box and on the witness stand. He procured jobs for them in different sections of the South.[5] It was natural that the newspapers should pin a great deal of hope on all of the general's utterances. His discussion of President Johnson's attitude delivered in the Brooklyn Academy of Music caused considerable comment. A report of General Fiske's speech read in part:

. . . Yesterday I had a talk with the President who said to me that he felt the great responsibility committed to him. 'People say, sometimes, I was born in the South, and I will not treat the negro as a free man, but I mean and desire to carry out the views of the Great American Lincoln, and to see that those people have a guarantee to their freedom. I may not believe with you in their ultimate attainments, but I mean they shall have a fair chance. I wish the people of

[5]*The South Carolina Leader*, October 14, 1865.

the North knew what I have to stand between. Daily I receive telegrams and letters from all parts of the South, of dreadful import. If they could but see the difficulties of my position, they would pity me and give me their prayers.' This he said with tears in his eyes; and I asked him if the Freedman's Bureau was to be discontinued, my resignation already in his hands—he said to me 'Go back, go to your work, and see justice done to both white and Black! The Freedman's Bureau will only cease to exist when the Southern States are resolved to deal honestly and justly by these freedmen.'[6]

One should bear in mind when reading this report that southern Blacks at that time distrusted southern whites in interracial affairs. Since the President was a native of the South, General Fiske attempted to break down this prejudice on the part of Blacks, and urged them to keep open minds about Johnson's administration. While the president attempted to appease the Blacks through General Fiske, he had also to face his southern white constituency, who looked upon him as the leader of their cause to re-establish their dominant position. Naturally, it appeared that his sympathetic attitude toward Blacks was inconsistent with his unrevoked role as leader of the southern whites.

Whatever ideas the president had in mind for reconciling his conflicting attitudes, his political enemies were active in thwarting his action. Thaddeus Stevens and Charles Sumner formed a strong political bloc among their colleagues to force action in Congress on the continuance of the Freedman's Bureau. The radical senators doubted Johnson's sympathy for Blacks and held that his refusal to approve the bill would prove that fact. Johnson did veto the bill and the *Colored Tennessean* was quick to make editorial comment. The newspaper endeavored to enlighten its readers on the necessity of having the government intervene during the transition to a new order. The statement made by the *Colored Tennessean* read in part:

. . . President Johnson has vetoed the bill known as the "Civil

---

[6]"The President and the Freemen," *The South Carolina Leader*, December 9, 1865.

Rights Bill," whose object was to secure to the colored men protection in person and property and not the elective franchise. The President enters into a rather lengthy discussion of the principles involved in the bill and finds many serious objections to it becoming law. It is yet to be determined whether the freedmen are to have any protection or whether they are to be left to the mercy of their enemies.[7]

In comparison with the storm of criticism that raged after the president's veto, the comment by the *Colored Tennessean* was mild.

The radical senators, in the meantime, had marshaled their forces and thus a second bill extending the bureau's life was passed over the president's veto. A report on the bill includes the following comment:

... the bill of 1866 did not merely provide for the care of freedom. It conferred sweeping jurisdiction upon the officers of the Bureau, who were authorized to take over many functions then belonging to state magistrates, and clerks, etc. ... One of the most striking features of the bill was that which established military jurisdiction under regulations issued through the Secretary of War over all cases concerning the immunities and rights of freedmen. This meant the seizure of an immense field of civil and criminal jurisprudence formerly belonging to the state courts and the transfer of such jurisdiction to the military courts.[8]

Acts by the army in their governing of local communities were not always beyond reproach. Some of the officers ruled with an iron fist and, in some cases, created unnecessary conflicts. They viewed situations always from the point of view of bending everyone to their will. An example of this despotic rule was pointed out by the New York *Tribune* when the army invoked the right of censorship of the press in South Carolina. The situation was precipitated when the editor of the *South Carolina Leader* made an editorial attack on the president and

---

[7]*The Colored Tennessean*, March 31, 1865.
[8]14 *United States Statutes at Large* 173 (Act of July 16, 1866).

was forced by the army to resign. Under the caption, "Loyalty and Freedom Squelched," an editorial in the New York *Tribune* commented on the incident:

... The South Carolina Leader, devoted to free labor and practical reform, found fault, as it was bound to do, with the President's veto of the Bureau bill, and still more so with his speech to the motley crew who serenaded him in the evening. The editor, Mr. A. Coffin, of Massachusetts, was induced to resign his desk after publishing the article upon the President's speech. Mr. Moore, a South Carolinian, was appointed in his place. Major-General Devens sent word to the editor that no more such articles would be published. The publisher reported that the writer of the obnoxious article had been removed and the President would be sustained hereafter. The new editor waited upon the General, and satisfied him that no case for complaint should again occur. Thus the rebel papers of Charleston are allowed to vilify and caricature Congress, but the loyal paper in the state must cease criticizing the President. The legislative power may be abused, but the executive must be screened by military authority.[9]

A bad feature in government control, from the Black's point of view, was seen in this interference by the army, which was effected on instructions from the president. By muzzling the press, the army violated one of the cardinal principles of democracy. Yet the *South Carolina Leader* was faced with submission to the will of the government or discontinuance of publication. Probably that accounts for the newspaper's weak editorial reply, which rationalized its position in this fashion:

... First, he [the editor of the New York *Tribune*] writes that the editor from Massachusetts, after writing a certain article, was induced to resign his desk and a South Carolinian appointed in his place. He was not induced to resign his desk for any such reason. He was aware that for weeks previous to his writing the article in question a change in

---

[9]New York *Tribune*, March 24, 1866.

the editorial department had been contemplated, owing to the fact that the proprietors of the Leader were desirous to reduce expenses and because the "Editor from Massachusetts" felt indisposed to labor for "the cause" at a salary deemed by him disproportionate to his service. He "didn't get enough of money".

2. General Devans never sent word to this office. . . .

3. The proprietor never reported that . . . the President would be supported . . . The Leader . . . is an enemy to slaver and all that pertains to it, and never will be else while we own interest in it. We are the friend of no one who would oppress his fellow being "because he is poor, because he is ignorant, or because he is Black". A man is a man for all that . . . Men are not northern loyalists nor southern rebels with us. They are all our fellow countrymen . . . they are our brothers and we will stand by all who love and honor our common country. We have no sympathy with those self-constituted martyrs who devote their time, a penny a line, to misrepresenting the white man or the Black man, North or South, for the purpose of raising a paper monument to the memory of fallen icons and have their pictures exhibited thereafter as "Champions of Liberty."[10]

Normally, and for all practical purposes, the Freedman's Bank was a part of the Freedmen's Bureau, although it had no legal connection. Indirectly, governmental influence gave a certain personal safety to the individual depositor since the bureau had a supervisory function over the bank. The importance of the bank was stressed by the Charleston *Journal* in explaining its advantages to the depositor:

. . . This bank is open for the reception of deposits for any one who may wish to put his money away for safe-keeping and at the same time get interest upon it. As some persons seem to think that this bank is designed for freedmen only, we would say that a savings bank not only saves one's money from thieves and plunderers, and from unnecessary spending and lavish by the possessor, but as soon as any amount is

---

[10]*The South Carolina Leader*, March 31, 1866.

deposited it begins to grow, increasing from the interest which is paid the depositor. By this means any amount of money in a certain length of time doubles itself, the amount of interest increasing in proportion as the amount first deposited is increased by other deposits. In this way many persons soon get rich. . . .[11]

However, government control was not the complete answer to the problem but served only as an auxiliary to the social process in accommodating the Blacks to the new social order.

VI. BLACK LEADERSHIP AND WHITE ESTEEM

The adjustment of the Black to the new social order depended upon not only government control but also the Black himself. One editor followed the editorial policy of urging Blacks, therefore, to strive for recognition as intellectuals, scientists, inventors, manufacturers, and mechanics.[1] The Black newspapers were especially alert and diligent in presenting distinctive successes of Blacks, so as to encourage others to imitate their action.

In printing detailed accounts of Blacks recognized in their communities as leaders and held in esteem by whites, Black newspapers emphasized the fact that their achievements had called for extreme personal sacrifices. To the Black press the individual was not important unless his accomplishments aided the development of other Blacks. Thus the Black was urged to feel a responsibility for the advancement of his group.

There were several instances of Black papers stressing the importance of economic advance. For example, the *South Carolina Leader* took pride in pointing out that a colored man was the highest bidder at the auction sale of two fine estates in Stanton, Virginia. The account of this man's progress encouraged others to try to follow his example, for they rightly felt that what one Black accomplished others might do.[2]

---

[11]Charleston *Journal*, October 11, 1866.

[1]*The Elevator*, June 21, 1867.

[2]*The South Carolina Leader*, December 9, 1865.

The *Elevator* pointed to striking cases of economic progress made by Blacks in Philadelphia. One story told that Stephen Smith had amassed a fortune of over $300,000 from the sale of lumber and from real estate operations. Another Black, Harris Lindsay, a bounty broker, was listed as being worth $250,000. The index to the social progress of the total Black population in Philadelphia and their estimated wealth was the number of churches supported by the group. The California paper stated that there were seventeen such churches.[3]

The editor of the *Virginia Star* wrote at length about his visit to the estate of W. P. Mosely, a state senator of Virginia, saying:

... We love to talk to such men of our race as Senator Mosely, for it is such characters as he in our midst that are needed to disprove the repeated accusation that the Negro is making no progress. Here he owns a beautiful plantation containing five hundred acres, a great portion under cultivation and well stocked. He has around him an intelligent and refined family circle, and his home gives evidence of the careful training that has been pursued by him. He has a daughter who performs admirably on the organ, and the old homestead of the former master has greatly improved under the shrewd management of the present owner who was once the slave.[4]

The fact that a Black could live in a community and become highly respected also brought forth editorial comment:

... Henry O. Remmington was a colored man of marked ability, and the citizens of New Bedford, Massachusetts, where he lived and died, will long remember him, as his business brought him in contact with many families. He was a soap maker by trade, and always had a good article for sale. He was an artistic taxidermist, and spent much of his time in preparing birds. The knowledge which he displayed of the feathery tribe was very remarkable. When Prof. O. S.

[3]*The Elevator*, June 21, 1867.
[4]*The Virginia Star*, May 14, 1878.

Fowler, the phrenologist, was giving public examinations in the city of New Bedford, Mr. Remmington was called upon the platform by the audience for examinations. The professor put his hand upon his head and said, 'This is a wonderful head; order is fully developed; his love of nature is intense, and if left to his own inclination, the classification of birds would be his pursuit, in which he would find the highest enjoyment.' He was a prominent associate in the earlier anti-slavery agitations in his vicinity and attracted all hearts to him as a great leader. Never ambitious save to help in the cause of human rights, he was less known in the North than he deserved to be—as a wise counsellor, a trusty friend, and a fearless advocate of the rights of man. His death, which occurred but a few years since, occasioned general lamentation throughout the city. The friends of freedom gave him a public burial from the Liberty Hall, where the funeral services were held, and the procession which followed his remains to their final resting place, was one of the largest funeral processions seen in southeast Massachusetts.[5]

Accomplishments of individuals in the field of art, education, and culture were important for the advancement of the Black. Consequently, the newspapers were eager to report with pride on careers in these fields. In Rome, Miss Edmonia Lewis, a Black sculptress, engaged the studio quarters formerly occupied by the great master, Canova, and Black papers hailed her achievement in study and work. Later, photographic copies of her two groups of statuary called "The Wedding of Hiawatha," executed in Rome, were sold in the office of the *Elevator*.[6]

The editor of the *New Orleans Weekly Louisianian* showed no modesty in telling of the accomplishment of a young Black artist. An important weekly magazine had opened its pages to his work. Probably the editor did not realize that the acceptance of the artist's sketch was the beginning of an increasing appreciation by daily newspapers for Blacks in the field of art. At that time, the Black editor did realize, however, that the

[5]*The South Carolina Leader*, December 16, 1865.
[6]*The Elevator*, June 21, 1867.

youth had raised the Blacks in the esteem of whites. The article in the weekly read in part:

> ... Harper's Weekly of January 11 contains an engraving "from a sketch by H. J. Lewis" of the accumulation of cotton at the Pine Bluff, Arkansas depot, caused by the close of navigation and the meager carrying facilities of the railroad from thence to the Mississippi. I think it should be made known that Mr. H. J. Lewis, the artist who drew the sketch, is a colored man, as it is important that the race should receive due credit for all the literary and artistic merit it possesses. Mr. Lewis is a young colored resident of Pine Bluff, of about 25 years of age, slender build, dark brown complexion, and has attained his skill in drawing by his own exertion without any instruction. He has produced fine crayon portraits of several prominent citizens of our state. That an untaught Arkansas colored boy should by his own exertion attain sufficient merit to gain recognition from a paper of such high standing as Harper's Weekly is, I think, a circumstance worthy of note.[7]

Academic achievements of Blacks were especially commended by the press. When the first Black woman was graduated from an advanced institution of learning, it was an occasion for the newspapers to tell of new strides taken by Blacks. Miss Fanny Jackson of Washington, D. C., was graduated from Oberlin (Ohio) College in the spring of 1865. In the fall, the weeklies were jubilant over the announcement, first carried in the Boston *Daily Transcript*, that the first colored student had been admitted to the freshman class at Harvard College. He was Richard T. Grenner, and the Black newspapers followed his career with interest throughout his life. In addition to serving as Dean of Liberal Arts Faculty at Howard University, he was for a time one of the editors of the Frederick Douglass's *National Era*.

When Black leaders or individuals who had made a success were not accorded the respect due them, the newspapers complained. In the spring of 1878, the Black newspapers voiced a

---

[7]*The New Orleans Weekly Louisianian*, February 1, 1879.

complaint against Hampton Institute,[8] one of the first industrial schools for Blacks in the South, founded by General Samuel C. Armstrong. The school's teachers were assailed for failing to give due recognition to Black professional men when
they visited the campus. Such disrespect was regarded as a
slight to the whole Black group. The Virginia school was often
visited by leading physicians, circuit elders, and ministers of
different denominations. The young white teachers apparently
put forth no effort to give them a welcome greeting. The teachers, coming as they did from the North, did not sense that the
Black leader was skeptical as to the sincerity of whites wherever they appeared. Under the old régime, the southern whites
never employed subtle devices of deceit in their dealings with
the Black—in fact, there was no need, for the southern
planter's word was law. Within a short time, the Blacks had
come to view northern whites with increasing distrust, since
the latter talked about equality and lack of prejudice but did
not treat the Black as equals. Therefore, the reports of the
Black clergymen about their treatment caused considerable
discussion.

The breaking point, however, came when the Rev. Henry M.
Turner, business manager of the *Recorder*, visited the campus
during the spring of 1878. Originally, he had come to the institute to consider placing his daughter in the school's dormitory.
The Rev. Turner wrote a pungent account of his visit, and
many of the papers reprinted the article, adding their own
editorial remarks. A part of the minister's letter read:

. . . It is a grand structure, spacious rooms, and every conve-
nience apparently that heart could wish, and cleanliness prevailed in every department I looked into. But during my two
hours stay, not a teacher asked me to sit down, made a soli-
tary explanation, gave me a welcome look, nor showed me
the civility of a visitor, while I was in the building. When I
would walk into the room, the teachers and students alike,
would throw a glance at me, and thus end their courtesies.
This was so different from the High School and University

---

[8]*The Virginia Star*, May 14, 1878.

manners at Scotia, Charlotte, Atlanta, Nashville, New Orleans, Jefferson, and indeed everywhere that I scarcely knew how to interpret it, except on the ground that 'we have no time to bother with you here'. Nevertheless, I noticed when white visitors came in chairs were offered them. . . .[9]

Black editors realized that if Blacks wanted to be treated with respect they should act so as to command respect, and therefore the press repeatedly gave instructions on behavior. The Athens *Blade* was a notable example of a weekly regularly carrying items relating to the conduct of Black people. The *Blade* was unusual in that one of its leading correspondents traveled extensively about the country in the performance of his regular profession. The correspondent wrote with remarkable ability, mixing wit and irony. So biting at times were his stories that it was well that he was known only as Uncle Jim Dudley. In giving instructions to Blacks as to how they should act, Uncle Dudley did not suggest that they conform to the social etiquette of the South. Uncle Dudley knew the etiquette of the South, which enables persons to act freely within the limits that the formal rules of personal relations impose, and has, perhaps, no higher sanction than the feeling of superiority one feels when one succeeds, or the sense of inferiority when one fails.[10]

In one of his releases Uncle Dudley gave implicit instructions how to deal with situations in public places. The report follows:

. . . The Madame and I took the 3 o'clock P. M. train over the Air Line railroad last Monday for this place. There was some objection made in our riding in the first class car from Athens, Georgia to Charlotte, but when I shelled up beside Mr. Conductor, and informed him that Mrs. Dudley was just as good as Mrs. Conductor and that Mr. Dudley would have crow-picking before she would ride in the smoking car, it was decided by all at hand that they had struck up with a couple of first class "nigger" passengers—that could ride

[9]*The Virginia Star*, May 11, 1878.
[10]Bertram W. Doyle, *The Etiquette of Race Relations in the South* (Chicago: University of Chicago Press, 1937), p. 5.

where they pleased. The old Lady and I gave ourselves rest and told the old train to go belching onward, which she did. . . .

I leave for Washington tomorrow. I am to get a peep at your Congressman and all the rest of them. I will let you know whether they should be retained or not.

Remember me to old Lux . . . tell them I am just as happy as a big sunflower, spending Mrs. Dudley's father's money.[11]

According to the principles advocated by the Black press, the responsibility of solving the problem of racial adjustment had to be shared by the individual Black. Eventually, the Black press said, the rise of Black leadership would cause whites to give up some of their old traditions.

VII. HOSTILITY AND SYMPATHY OF SOUTHERN WHITES: THE REACTION OF THE BLACK PRESS

A paradox in race relations existed during Reconstruction because the process necessary to adjust the Black in the new social structure gave rise to both hostility and sympathy on the part of whites.

There were whites in the South who showed sympathy for Blacks, but they were not always motivated by the sort of sympathy that made them attempt to understand and feel for the other person.[1] In fact, the sympathy generally demonstrated by whites for Blacks did two things. First, it made the Blacks look up to whites for protection; and, secondly, it exalted the superior feeling of whites over Blacks. It was a subtle and perhaps not always conscious social control exerted by whites to keep Blacks in a submissive position.

Naturally, there was also sympathy without ulterior motives

---

[11]*Athens Blade*, January 16, 1880.
[1]Edgar T. Thompson, *Race Relations and the Race Problem*, pp. 152-179.

in rendering assistance to Blacks. It was based on the recognition of democracy as applied to racial relationships; that is, on the acceptance of the change brought about by the Civil War. Among southern whites there were some genuine in this sense. They realized that Blacks needed economic security to take their first step toward racial adjustment, and some of them often even went so far as to leave their entire fortunes to colored friends.[2]

Individuals manifesting genuine sympathy for Blacks, however, were subjected to bitter attack; for in the opinion of the masses of southern whites, the Black was not a human being and, consequently, it was useless to think of him in sympathetic terms. The fact that Senator Ben Wade of Ohio exhibited strong sympathy for Blacks caused southerners to criticize him severely after his death. Because of the senator's prominence, the whites feared that his opinions might endanger the southern ideology of white supremacy. It was pointed out by a defender of Wade that

> ... In the Recorder of the 9th inst., appeared an article headed "Ben Wade", in which my judgment you unwarrantably assailed the dead patriot and statesman, whose memory is dear to me, if not others in Georgia and I deem it a duty I owe truth and justice to make some reply to your main aspersion upon his character.
>
> Referring to the statement of Senator Wade that he would refuse to arrest and return to his master under the fugitive slave law, a Negro running away from slavery, you say: "The above is characteristic of men such as Wade and those who thought like him" and that "Mr. Wade was a bitter partisan and a hater of the South". Let me say to you, that Senator Wade did not hate the white people of the South, but with hundreds and thousands of others in the North, as well as in the South, hated the accursed institution of slavery. For many years of his great and useful life he had made it a study and understood it thoroughly, and the dangers with which its continued existence menaced the country. He denounced slavery as a crime when from thousands of pulpits

---

[2]*Athens Blade*, February 20, 1880.

it was declared to be a divine institution. Impressed with the truth of his convictions, he supported them with earnestness born of sincerity. He hated the fugitive slave law that made northern freemen the partners of southern bloodhounds, that called it a crime to give a cup of cold water or crust of bread to a human being endeavoring to regain his birthright of freedom.[3]

Wade's motive was clearly explained, but the southern whites resented attitudes that seemingly weakened their belief in white supremacy.

A similar resentment was seen, on one occasion, when General Grant was touring the South. It happened that

> ... The hotel keeper in Jacksonville, when General Grant was entering the hotel in that place, attempted to prevent the colored people from entering. General Grant turned to him and said, "Wherever I am, they can come."[4]

Philanthropic efforts of northern whites were another cause for hostility in the South, and the Black was caught in the center of a wedge made by the bitter sectional feeling. Carloads of provisions, according to the press, were sent to Blacks. Northern philanthropy made Blacks independent of the dominant group. Perhaps this antagonized the South because the act would seem to indicate that they were being forced into a position to accept a new social relationship with Blacks. Naturally, this embittered the southern whites; and, in retaliation against the Yankees, they displayed hatred toward the Blacks.

Southern whites not only resented that type of sympathy, but as a result became even more hostile in their attitude toward Blacks. In other words, the whites became determined to assert more vigor in establishing race relations along caste lines. The South did not want to give up its mores and traditions, despite political and social pressure from the North.

Another condition that resulted in hostility toward the Blacks was the differences in treatment of the Blacks shown

---

[3]*Ibid.*, February 27, 1880.
[4]*Ibid.*, February 6, 1880.

by the major political parties. Since the Republicans of the North had reversed the position of Blacks, the native southerners remained loyal adherents to the Democratic party. Republicans endorsed the active participation of Blacks in their conventions and included them on their ballots for elective offices. The admission of an egalitarian position for Blacks was a severe wound to southern traditions and ideals. Thus, action on the part of Republicans was challenged by Democrats, and hostility toward Blacks mounted. In Camden County, Georgia, it was stated:

> . . . There are Democrats here, who are extreme in politics; they are not willing to accord the Negro every right the law guarantees him; but there is a perplexing and pestilent policy, a southern Democratic prototype, that was bred out of the lost cause; declaration to rule on any scale, at any rate, rather than be ruled or associated with men of color. It was this policy that made the good white citizens of St. Mary's refuse to sign a petition which . . . was gotten up by Hon. Thomas Butler, the Negro representative to the legislature, asking the repeal of an unconstitutional law (the law authorizing the governor to appoint Mayor and Aldermen for the town of St. Mary's.)[5]

Danger that political activity would assimilate Blacks and whites caused the white Democrats to oppose Republican principles and led the Republicans to do little to carry out those principles, which theoretically guaranteed the political rights of the Black. For instance, in one county it was stated:

> . . . We have a Republican County Executive Committee composed of long-tried, honest and staunch Republicans. . . . We have a large Republican majority and can elect a Republican any election we choose in the county, and yet we don't fill but one of the county offices aside from Representative. This is because we are too poor to give bond; it is hoped that this obstacle will soon be removed, as our people are accumulating property fast.[6]

[5]*Ibid.*, October 31, 1879.
[6]*Ibid.* (Letter to Editor).

Blacks competing for offices that whites demanded for themselves also aroused hostility.[7] The Democrats held white Republicans, especially in the North, responsible for the political ambitions of Blacks and when elected to office, the southerners claimed, the Blacks became puppets of individual white men.

Another illustration of sharp racial conflict was seen in the dramatic action of President Johnson when the editor of the *Tennessean* interviewed him and, at the same time, solicited a subscription to his paper. Before commenting, the president looked over the list of subscribers about Washington, and, on observing that Senator Sumner had contributed five dollars, Johnson signed his name directly under that of his political enemy for five times the sum contributed by the senator.[8] The conflict between the North and the South was ripe at every turn, and the Black found himself between the cross fire.

Although the Black press was concerned about the social adjustment of the Black and agitated to bring about his integration into the new order, the stand on the question of limited suffrage that some of the papers took at the beginning of the Reconstruction period merely resulted in widening the gap between the whites and the Blacks. The newspapers insisted that limited suffrage would be unprofitable to the Blacks and ineffective in improving race relations. The papers contended that under a program of limited suffrage. oppressive law could be instituted with greater facility than under a program of total suffrage for the Black, and therefore the adjustment process would be hindered.[9]

Skepticism had arisen as to the willingness of the South to make some adjustment to the Black, and the press apparently did not anticipate the stubborn refusal of whites to accommodate the Black, at least to an appreciative degree. The *Elevator* stated that it was a mistake to think that the South would forget mores that had existed for three centuries; for, the newspaper stated:

> . . . That the numerous great families which have been ruined in the late fierce struggle, should sit down content with

[7]Francis Butler, *South Carolina During Reconstruction*, p. 355.
[8]*The South Carolina Leader*, May 12, 1866.
[9]*The Charleston Journal*, October 4, 1866.

any terms they can now expect, does not seem quite as likely as that they will remain moody and acrimonious, rebels at heart; that the soldiery shall be transformed like Cromwell's, into peaceable and industrious citizens is not very probable; for we know that even Cromwell's soldiers were ready to rise up, had they a leader. . . .[10]

While the Black press realized that better social conditions, caused by the occupation of the army, could not create an ideal democracy, it foresaw that the withdrawal of troops meant the complete denial of suffrage to Blacks. The press also felt that government control was necessary for the protection of the Freedmen's Bureau. Of the need of the army's protection, the Charleston *Journal* reminded the governor of a southern state:

. . . If he happened to be anywhere in South Carolina when hostilities ceased, he knows full well how confused the state of affairs was, not knowing where to go or what to do. It was necessary that the Bureau or something similar should quiet and settle them and organize and enforce some system of labor, which the Bureau did and is still enforcing admirably.[11]

The press realized that objective political leadership was necessary, for race relations in the South were such that one paper expressed a fear that the situation would be worse for the Black "than that of the English landlord in Tipperary, for there at least the administration of the laws is not in possession of the same class who shoots at him while passing along the highway, or burns his house over his head.[12]

One man whom the Black press did not regard as a good leader was B. F. Perry, the provisional governor of South Carolina. Apparently, he did not possess the prerequisites for tasks that called for an astute politician who could objectively direct Blacks and whites in a new relationship. He was an illustrious example of a person yielding to the mores instead of upholding

---

[10]*The Elevator*, May 5, 1865.
[11]Charleston *Journal*, October 4, 1866.
[12]*The Elevator*, May 5, 1865.

the political will of the national government. The Charleston *Journal* sharply criticized Perry because of his indifference to the race adjustment problem. Perry exposed his reactionary attitude when a northern white group invited him to address an audience in New York City and he declined. The Charleston *Journal* reacted unfavorably to the governor's declination; for it felt that since he was a representative of the state government, his act would encourage the extension of southern hostility. According to the *Journal* the governor's action

. . . did neither himself nor his country any good. In these times when the social and political elements are so combustible, the torch should be carefully avoided.[13]

The Black press accused the South of rebelling against the federal government, and disseminated ideas as presented by the North, censuring whites for not taking the initiative in accommodating the Black to the new social structure. Possibly, it was for this reason that the Charleston *Journal* said of Perry:

. . . He says nothing to mitigate the guilt of his state, he throws no light upon reconstruction, nor will his letter (referring to the letter declining the invitation to speak) assist his state to renew its Federal relation, but it is evidence to convince the North that the South is not prepared to resume that relationship. It seems to us to be but the belching forth of hate towards the colored people, and a spirit of war, and we confess our regret that this letter breathes no spirit of philanthropy or peace.[14]

In addition to challenging political practices of whites, newspapers ridiculed "defensive beliefs" utilized by whites to retain their superior social position. "Defensive beliefs" is a term used by John Dollard to explain how southern whites rationalize their action in discriminating against the Black. Among the Black editors, some had traveled in Europe and had seen

---

[13]Charleston *Journal*, October 4, 1866.
[14]*Ibid.*

Blacks accepted on the same intellectual basis as whites. Therefore, Black editors refuted the contention that mental differences stood in the way of a harmonious relationship between Blacks and whites. One of the editors cited high attainments of Africans in letters and science to prove that color should not be the basis for judging mental capacities of the two races. He commented on the question:

> . . . is the Negro by nature equal to the white man, mentally and physically? If the white man should make this remark to learned and scientific men in England or France, he would be laughed at. Many native born Africans attend academies and colleges in England, and there are instances upon record in which they have excelled the sons of high Englishmen.[15]

On this same question, the intelligence of Blacks, the *Missionary Record* pointed out that people of every generation had recognized statesmen, philosophers, and warriors because of their achievements, and in no case on account of race or color.[16] The paper claimed:

> . . . We have observed that all civilized nations honor their men of learning. But we observe that in this State learning is the greatest means of disqualification, especially among colored men . . . it is lamentable that the meanest, and most unpricipled white men with no reputation, with no education, may occupy the highest position among colored people and their words are received as oracular declarations. The more brazen, the more honor conferred; the more unscrupulous, the better qualified to lead these new-made citizens.[17]

Besides deploring the false assertion about the mental differences between Blacks and whites, the Black papers complained of the hostility shown by the southern white churches. Since religion has the power to arouse the emotions of men, the Black editors expected that the church leaders would also endorse

---

[15]*Ibid.*
[16]*The Missionary Record*, August 26, 1871.
[17]*Ibid.*

the proposal, as many Blacks, seeking freedom, had already escaped from their masters and had joined the Union army. Planters took steps to check the exodus by having slaves conscripted as army laborers, but the first victory of a northern army gave Lincoln the occasion to issue the Emancipation Proclamation. Thus the dominant agricultural civilization was reduced in its position. Lincoln was among the first to discover that

> ... the emancipation policy and the aid of colored troops constituted the severest blow yet dealt to the rebellion, and that at least one of these important successes could not have been achieved when it was, but for the aid of Black soldiers.[18]

The proclamation brought a storm of criticism from England because the dominant classes there favored the Confederacy, which believed in free trade, as opposed to the North, which favored high tariff. Among those who approved of the proclamation were the organized laborers of Europe. As a correspondent to the "New York Tribune," Karl Marx had followed the situation carefully, before and during the rebellion. He had been firm in advocating emancipation as the only way of uprooting the evil forces disastrous to organized labor.

When the war ended, all the slaves in the United States had been declared free, either by the Emancipation Proclamation or state action, except those in Delaware and Kentucky, for these two states had not seceded. The Thirteenth Amendment, which ensured the freedom of the former slaves, automatically freed the slaves in Delaware and Kentucky.

Before the end of the war Lincoln had formulated a plan of Reconstruction, or readjustment of the seceded states to the federal government. He had assumed that the responsibility of making adjustments for humanitarian goals would be set up for the social conduct of its members. In this endeavor the southern churches failed, for they sanctioned the old traditions. The churches are characterized thus:

---

[18]Carl Schurz, *Abraham Lincoln: The Gettysburg Speech and Other Papers by Abraham Lincoln* (New York: Houghton Mifflin Co., 1878), p. 68.

. . . Instead of exercising a spirit of conciliation and Christian forbearance, hate has been their watchword. They ransacked their brains to find newfangled oaths with which to curse Yankees and Negroes, and the blows intended for others have rebounded upon their own heads, and their curses, like chickens, have come back to roost.[19]

In the face of all the hostility, one Black newspaper tried to show that it was to the advantage of each social group to respect the rights of the other, as a successful adjustment was not possible as long as either group felt persecuted. The paper stated:

. . . Many whites forget that we have the interest of Georgia as much at heart as any other class of citizens in it. Our mission is to make the two races feel that each is at home, and that each has a work to do that will promote the other. Many of our white citizens don't feel that way . . . If we could once lead the whites of our country to see that we are their friends, and that we wish to labor with them to do honor to Georgia, all would be well.[20]

The Black press endeavored to break down arguments presented by whites to prove racial differences, and was very loyal to the Republican party, which opposed the old southern traditions. But the press accomplished very little in its attempt to better race relations throughout the South. It did not fail, however, to point out the harm caused by the malicious character of propaganda, which seriously hampered the racial adjustment of Blacks and whites.

Southern propagandists appealed to the emotions of whites by indulging in generalities about Blacks. This was a useful weapon in uniting whites in unfavorable attitudes toward Blacks. So useful was this technique that the *New Orleans Semi-Weekly Louisianian* claimed that it obstructed progress in racial adjustment. The newspaper stated:

---

[19]Charleston *Journal*, October 4, 1866.
[20]Athens *Blade*, October 31, 1879.

. . . The trump card of the old system was a fat, sleepy and professedly contented slave. Such a specimen was always on hand to be exhibited to the unbelieving Yankee or Britisher when they came South. The trump card is now an extravagant legislator. He is pointed out as a bond-bloated and warrant-stuffed specimen of Reconstruction—the accursed thing of the 15th Amendment.[21]

Generalities of this type suggested that illiterate Blacks, as pawns of the Yankees, were assuming a superior position over whites. Thus it was a factor in arousing the emotions of southern whites. These notions took on a stereotyped form, and the technique was simplified. Names used to identify these stereotypes influenced whites who formed their judgment without analyzing the evidence presented. For example, this was seen when the *New Orleans Weekly Louisianian* erroneously referred to a white newspaper as being among its colored exchanges. The white paper, demanding a correction of the mistake, called the Black editor "blue gum"—a name used to convey a stereotyped idea held by whites. The white newspaper stated:

. . . We agree with our contemporary that it is not a crime to be a colored man but as the political record of so many of them is anything but enviable by an honorable gentleman this is what makes it the more objectionable. "Blue gum" is the name of an ex-statesman, colored at that, to whose fingers other people's money "make fast" and cannot be extricated, except by the use of a horsewhip, as was done by a cab driver at the Fair grounds.[22]

The primary aim of the white editor was to berate Blacks for giving evidence of their ability to think along the same lines as whites. To make his biased opinion effective, the white editor raised, through a name, an idea suggesting that Blacks were dishonest by nature. Blacks had been painted with hat in hand, grinning and displaying blue gums, while talking to

---

[21]*The New Orleans Semi-Weekly Louisianian,* June 15, 1871.
[22]*The New Orleans Weekly Louisianian,* March 27, 1880.

whites. Therefore, it was not difficult to convert "blue gum" into a useful propaganda weapon.

A different technique was used to destroy ideas that Blacks had any resemblance to whites, by circulating stories that Blacks were savages planning a white massacre. Fear was a strong force in controlling attitudes of whites. One Black editor called attention to this type of propaganda and claimed:

... The Choctaw Courier is indulging in vain attempts at justification. This miserable sheet would have the people of the country believe that the colored people have become so indifferent to their own welfare and of those among whom they live, so bloodthirsty and blackhearted, that they would deliberately plot against the lives of thousands of whites. The respectable public will not shake the blood-stained hands of the Choctaw editor nor permit him to deceive them as to the real object of the murder. . . . it only shows the vile animus and wickedness of its editor.[23]

Such ideas, creating fear, withheld facts so as to reduce possibilities of an amicable racial adjustment. In the same manner, the technique of overemphasizing facts was used to produce the same result. This was seen in an editorial appearing in the *Sentinel*, a white newspaper. The statement, reprinted in a black newspaper, read:

... 'What we need is encouragement, not curses; protection, not violence.'
We clip the above from the N. O. Weekly La. . . . edited, owned and printed by Niggers who sent us a copy asking an exchange with the Sentinel. We will grant the gentlemanly darkies the boon they crave, that they may study African ethnology from a stalwart standpoint.
'What we need is encouragement, not curses; protection, not violence.' That is the Nigger all over. Why, you great wooly-headed boobies, what you need is to learn to 'curse' and practice 'violence' and all these other things will be added to you. If you have not enough sand to stand up and curse

---

[23]*People's Advocate*, September 25, 1876.

the lantern-jawed brigadiers and the white-livered retainers, then the Republican Party made a great mistake in giving you your freedom. If these unhung traitors dare molest you when you go to vote, shoot them as you would so many dogs. If you have not the courage to do so, get on the auction block and let them sell you to the highest bidder.

—A six-shooter is what you need, Mr. Nig... [24]

To have followed this advice would have been disastrous for Blacks because what appeared on the surface to be a challenge was propaganda. Rash action on the part of Blacks would have substantiated arguments for extending caste barriers.

In a tone of sarcasm, the *New Orleans Weekly Louisianian* tried to reduce the value of propaganda ideas presented by its contemporaries. On the subject of "blue gum," the paper stated:

... By and by, who in the deuce is 'blue gum'? Is he active or an ex-statesman, and where does he live or claim to live? A 'blue gum' is a rare bird; we would like to have the identity of such a unique character given to us. He does not belong to that species of 'rare birds' with which you are pleased to classify him, for he resembles the buzzard more than another kind. He is a native of some portion of the North of this country and once and still claims his residence here but it's 'no go' now. He had trampled all over the country during the Centennial year; shortly after his return 'home' was financially busted and politically damned. He once travelled with a nigger minstrel, beating the tambourines, and this is possibly where he has learned to perfection the art of 'beating other people out of their just due', ourselves for instance, to the tune of upwards of $600. [25]

The Athens *Blade* complained about the editorial policy of the Atlanta *Constitution*, one of the largest white dailies of the South at that time. The Black journal accused the daily of spreading hostile attitudes and warned that there was danger

---

[24]*The New Orleans Weekly Louisianian*, August 9, 1879.
[25]*Ibid.*, March 27, 1879.

in fanning the flame of hatred. The Black newspaper was striving to soften the tension in race feeling so that Blacks would be accorded better treatment. The Athens *Blade* reviewed the situation by recalling

> . . . the language of the press and the speeches of the day, and see how we were detested and scorned for availing ourselves of the rights which we then acquired. And though there is some abatement of that violence, it has not wholly passed away. The leaders of the convention of 1877 which framed the present constitution of Georgia, on the floor of that body, described the colored people as 'five thousand savages' and has lost nothing in popularity and power by that outrageous imputation.[26]

While attributing all the unfavorable acts to the spirit of slavery, the Athens *Blade* asserted that slavery was bygone and prevailed upon the Atlanta *Constitution* to reverse its policy. The Black press held that the white newspapers had to assist in bringing about an adjustment of Blacks in the new social order. Once their effort became mutual, the Black editor contended, all would be well.[27]

Perhaps the cause was not entirely hopeless, for one white newspaper in the deep South complained about the malicious propaganda circulated to arouse dissension. This publication stated:

> . . . We can only say to our friends as we have so often said to them before, have nothing to do with anything which appeals to you as a separate race. Be sure that when anyone claims your business or your vote on the score of color he has designs on you for his good and not your own, and if you let him severely alone you will be doing yourself a service.[28]

"Defensive beliefs" and propaganda were used to safeguard

---

[26]Athens *Blade*, October 31, 1879.
[27]*Ibid.*
[28]*The New Orleans Weekly Louisianian*, August 9, 1879. (Reprint from the Natchez *Democrat and Courier*.)

the old mores and traditions of the South. The propagandists appealed to the emotions through generalities, influenced minds by withholding facts, overemphasized situations so as to evade facts, and created stereotypes for degrading all Blacks. The Black press did not fail, however, to point out the harm caused by the malicious character of propaganda, while at the same time working for the racial adjustment of Blacks and whites.

VIII. STRATEGY FOR SURVIVAL

The years following 1880 were to be different and difficult, for the Blacks had to cope with the resistance to change on the part of whites, to educate the great mass of Blacks for a new civilization, to reconcile new patterns with old traditions, and to fight for the rights of Blacks even to the point of survival.

Booker T. Washington, who achieved worldwide fame as the head of Tuskegee Institute, Tuskegee, Alabama, was the foremost strategist among Blacks during this period. Washington overshadowed in prominence every other Black leader in America and was the first to receive the mantle of leadership from whites. Of course, he was the center of sharp criticism from Black leaders who opposed his policy; which was one of compromise.

Conditions under which Washington had lived during his childhood and young manhood must be considered in the evaluation of his philosophy. He was a product of the slave culture. He feared that the hostile attitude of southern whites could not be approached with a direct demand for political and social justice without accentuating their bitterness. His philosophy of compromise advocated gradualism for the Black in attaining his full rights of citizenship.

In developing Tuskegee Institute, Washington molded his philosophy. It called upon Blacks to accept the plan of a complete separation of the two races. It called upon whites to give Blacks work opportunities. It asked Blacks to give up an aggressive course for political and social rights. It asked of whites to give Blacks an opportunity for industrial education. It prevailed upon Blacks to remain in the South and to train in technical trades. It prevailed upon whites to recognize the skilled ability of Blacks and to make use of their services. In short, Washington's compromise was a plan of strategy for gaining a period of time so greatly needed for Black education.

Washington's critics wanted an outright stand for full economic, political, and social justice. They were not willing to concede the idea of separation as a harmonious pattern of communal living. The critics contended that the laws of economics would not reconcile segregation and equality for Blacks.

Outstanding among Washington's critics was W. E. B. DuBois. By birth and training he was the direct opposite of Washington. DuBois was born in Great Barrington, Mass., and could trace his ancestry back to the French Huguenots on his father's side and colonial Dutch on his mother's side. Washington could only surmise about his birth, for he never knew his father. DuBois received years of university training, including Fisk, Harvard, and Berlin. Washington barely squeezed into a manual training school by proving he could clean a classroom thoroughly. DuBois taught for a short time in a rural section of the South, later in universities. In between the years of teaching, he founded and edited the *Crisis* magazine, wrote books and engaged in scholarly research in Black life. Washington established in the wilderness of Alabama, Tuskegee Institute, known all over the world for its leadership in industrial education. DuBois, the scholar, looked to the future. Washington, the educator, lived from day to day.

Another severe critic of Washington's philosophy was William Monroe Trotter, publisher of the Boston *Guardian*. From the fall of 1903 until his death some years ago, Lucius Harper, executive of the Chicago Defender, wrote in his column "Dustin' off the News", March 2, 1946, Trotter edited the *Guardian*, utilizing it as a "front line trench" against the invasion of Dr. Washington's principles and policies in the North. Harper's account of Trotter said:

Trotter was born in Chillicothe, Ohio, in 1871. His father, James Monroe Trotter, fought in the 54th Massachusetts colored regiment during the Civil War, served as clerk in the Boston post-office, wrote a book on early day Negro musicians and singers entitled: "Music and Some Musical People." He was Recorder of Deeds in President Grover Cleveland's first administration. The position then carried no stated salary and it was said that Trotter's fees netted around $40,000 while he held the post.

William Monroe Trotter was reared in Hyde Park, Mass. He attended a white church and his associates in his high school and college days were largely white. He received his A.B. degree from Harvard in 1895 with a Magna Cum Laude and two years later got his M.A. degree. He entered into the real estate business with a white partner, did well and lived in a palatial home in aristocratic Sawyer Avenue before he launched the (Boston) Guardian, a weekly paper, in the fall of 1901. With Trotter's education and environment, there was very little about him that was in harmony with Booker Washington and his ideas. But he made no open protest until the fall of 1901 when he determined that the sage of Tuskegee was carrying his industrial program a little too far and with dangerous results. When Washington said "that it was more important that a gentlemanly Negro and not a bestial Negro rode in a Jim Crow car than that there were Jim Cars" that Trotter took to the open field to oppose him, declaring that such a statement definitely approved a caste system. He dug into Washington's record and found that he had somewhat sanctioned disfranchisement of the Negro to gain southern favor and enhance his industrial program. He declared that Washington should operate his school and not attempt to be "the voice of the Negro" to the detriment of the race's social progress in both North and South.

At a public meeting in Boston in 1901 Trotter blasted Booker T. for his utterances on disfranchisement and Jim Crow cars, raking him fore an aft. In return the two white dailies of that city shelled Trotter. The Boston Transcript said "Trotter is an example of an over-educated Negro." The Boston Herald declared: "Trotter shows that education does not always give a Negro good sense." Both papers refused to print Trotter's reply, and it was then that he saw the need for a mouthpiece to oppose the onrush of Washington's policies in the North: he launched the Boston Guardian with

95

George W. Forbes as editor and himself business manager. They broke friendship, however, after the "Boston Riot" in the summer of 1903 when Trotter spent 30 days in the Charles street jail for breaking up a meeting in the Columbus Avenue AME church being addressed by Dr. Washington. He interrupted the speaker with torrid questions regarding his policies on disfranchisement and Jim Crow cars, and so disturbed the meeting that it ended in a debacle. A riot call was sent in and twenty-five policemen responded, clearing the hall. Trotter was arrested.

What made the Black's plight extremely difficult was the lack of favorable publicity. The Black was generally misrepresented and pictured in a bad light by white periodicals and newspapers. It was suggested that

. . . editorials published against the Negro, which either ignore or minimize his good deeds and magnify his evil traits while they make heroes of our rapists and murderers, are for the prime business of creating sentiment against the Negro, which will eventually have as its end the consignment of the Negro to an indifferent place in the nation's esteem. Every bold headline of an article on the Negro which tells of the murder or some other despicable crime committed is a sentiment-maker against him.[1]

Frederick Douglass, the militant champion of abolition of slavery, had seen his better days and his last hope for gaining full citizenship for Blacks in the Black press. He felt that the strategy of the Black newspapers during the new epoch should be

. . . to say less about race and claims of race recognition, and more about the principles of justice, liberty, and patriotism. The press should say more of what we ought to do for ourselves and less about what Government ought to do for us;

---

[1]I. Garland Penn and J. E. E. Bowen, *The United Negro; His Problems and His Progress*, Atlanta, Ga.; D. E. Luther Publishing Co., 1902, p. 565.

more in the interest of morality and economy, and less in the interest of office-getting; more in commending the faithful and unflexible men who stand up for our rights, . . . an arrogant assumption for the colored man. . . .[2]

Douglass published his newspaper in the interest of the Black masses, but his readers were mostly northern whites engaged in the abolitionist movement and Europeans interested in the revolutionary spirit brewing in America. When the war between the states led to emancipation, Douglass' career as an editor was approaching its end. His energy and great power as an orator and writer had been spent without reservation during the decade before the Civil War.

After the Reconstruction period the newspapers were read more extensively by the Black masses. This is understandable, for during the slave economy the Blacks were denied the simplest form of education; they were not permitted to learn how to read and write.

Although the majority of Black leaders recognized the social importance of the newspapers, they also saw some inherent weaknesses that needed attention. It was generally agreed that the Black newspapers had printed a sufficient number of reports about their race to stimulate a growing pride among many Blacks. They had succeeded in molding public opinion to a certain extent, and they began the long haul in encouraging Blacks to take up and succeed in the arts and sciences.

The Age of Fortune
The elder statesman was a precursor to the first outstanding Black newspaper editor after Reconstruction—T. Thomas Fortune. Fortune definitely marked the first period of the Black press in the sense of modern journalism. At the time of the emancipation he was about ten years old and during the Reconstruction he had seen the flickering light of democracy. He really began where Douglass left off.

It was Fortune's opinion that the Black was confronted with as many drawbacks and hazards following the Reconstruction

---

[2]I. Garland Penn, *Afro-America Press* (Springfield, Mass.: Wiley & Co. Publishers, 1891) pp. 448-450.

period as those that had faced him on the eve of emancipation. He understood that:

> If the Negro did not carry with him in his face a proclamation of his race and previous condition of servitude . . . , a half-century would have sufficed to obliterate from the minds of men the fact that slavery once prevailed . . . , and the slaves were now free and citizens, equal under the Constitution and before the laws and other citizens of the country; but the mark of color remains and makes its possessor a pariah, to be robbed, beaten and lynched,—and a political nondescript, who has got his own salvation to work out, of equality before the laws with almost the entire white population of the country arrayed against him. Surely, no race of people ever had a larger job on their hands than have the colored citizens of the United States. The older they grow, the larger the job will become. . . . Already we are in the fury and heat of the conflict, but thousands of us do not know it, or, knowing it take no heed of the awful fact . . . It is here that the black press sustains to the black problem. . . . The newspaper has become . . . the oracle of the people. More than that it has become the defender of the just rights of the people against the encroachments of the ambitious and the covetous few. . . . The people are true to the editors only just as long as the editors are true to the people. As a regrettable fact, the white press of the South is leagued against the Black and his rights, and it is reinforced by nearly two-thirds of the press of the North and West . . .
> —The colored newspapers of the United States, some one hundred and twenty-five, are the only papers that are making a square, honest fight for the rights of our race. Not one of them receives the support it deserves; and, mainly on that account, not one is doing the work it could and should do.[3]

As a child, Fortune had seen his father assert his political rights in Florida, and from his parent he had acquired an independence of spirit and a consciousness of the problems facing the Black in a new civilization. Fortune's race consciousness,

---

[3]Penn, *Afro. American Press*, pp. 479-483.

a demand for respect as a citizen, appears as a reflection in every undertaking during his entire life. Some of his intimate friends regarded him as somewhat temperamental and impulsive in his later years. Yet, he never yielded his ground on issues involving the egalitarian position of the Black.

In his youth Fortune worked as a printer's devil in the office of the (Jacksonville, Florida) *Daily Union* after school hours. That was the beginning of his training in journalism. Ambitious to advance, Fortune secured for a time a job as clerk and rural mail carrier in the post office at Jacksonville. Conflict with the local postmaster on an issue involving respect on the same terms as whites caused him to quit. A year later, in 1875, he received an appointment as special inspector of customs for the first district of Delaware. Even this position did not satisfy his desire to be active in politics; at the time politics was at the core of Blacks' struggles for recognition as citizens. He resigned to take a teacher's training course at Howard University, the institution in Washington, D.C., supported by the federal government. For a short period he taught school and then found himself in the sphere of activity that meant a broad political life. From a position as compositor on the (New York) *Witness* he entered a partnership with George Parker and William Walter Sampson and with them founded the New York (weekly) *Globe* in 1882. But two years later, the partnership dissolved and the *Globe* was suspended. With his own social philosophy rapidly crystallizing, Fortune lost no time. In less than two weeks he brought out his New York *Freeman*.

Fortune started out with an awareness of all the criticisms that had been made about the more than two hundred journalistic efforts by Blacks since emancipation. These journalistic efforts had, for the most part, been failures. He was determined to make his a success. The typographical makeup of his sheet had balance and an attractive arrangement. He was an excellently trained printer, and the *Freeman* was the first newspaper to have a modern newspaper plant. Fortune's concern for the mechanical appearance of the *Freeman* did not cause him to neglect the quality of its editorial content. He employed capable assistants and sought contributions from writers from various sections of the country. Above all, the Fortune spirit—independence, perseverance, and courage—was to manifest itself in the editorial columns. He thought out clearly what he considered should be the Black's strategy in his new position. As he put it,

> I may stand alone in the opinion that the best interests of the race, and the best interests of the country will be conserved by building up a bond of union between the white people and the Negroes of the South, advocating the doctrine that the interests of the whites and the interests of the blacks are one and the same; that the legislation which affects the one will affect the other; that the good which comes to the one should come to the other; and that as one people the evils which blight the hopes of the one blight the hopes of the other. I say, I may stand alone among colored men in the belief that harmony of sentiment between the blacks and whites of the country, in so forth as it tends to honest division and healthy opposition, is natural and necessary, but I speak that which is a conviction as strong as the stalwart idea of diversity between the black and the white which has so crystallized the opinion of the race. It is not safe in the republican form of government that clannishness should exist either by compulsory or voluntary reason. It is not good for the government and it is not good for the individual. . . .
>
> The colored man is in the South to stay there. He will not leave it voluntarily and he cannot be driven out . . . the black population cannot and will not be dispensed with, because it is so deeply rooted in the South that it is a part of it—the most valuable part—and the time will come when it will hold to its title to the land, by right of purchase, for a laborer is worthy of his hire, and is now free to invest that labor as it pleases him best.[4]

Fortune was endeavoring to chart the principles by which Blacks could reconcile whites to accept their new status. How far this new idea was accepted cannot be proved, but it is not farfetched to suggest that Booker T. Washington may have found the essence of his famous Atlanta (Georgia) Exposition

---

[4]Simmons, *Men of Mark*, pp. 789-790.

speech in this expressed opinion of Fortune. The editor antici-
pated that such a view would meet with resentment on the
part of Blacks, and certainly Washington's statement of compromise

> Cast down your bucket where you are . . . In all things that
> are purely social we can be as separate as the fingers, yet
> one as the hand in all things essential to mutual progress . . .

caused a wide gulf in the opinion of northern Blacks, who were
against a philosophy of gradualism that accepted segregation
as a necessary step in attaining full citizenship. At this time
Fortune was the most influential Black in America and Washington enlisted his aid in publicizing Tuskegee. They became
good friends. Since Fortune was frequently in financial difficulties, he borrowed from the educator. Later Washington took
over Fortune's newspaper interest.

As an editor, Fortune's influence was given an interesting
test on an occasion when he went into a downtown salon in
New York City and the bartender crashed the beer glass after
Fortune had finished his drink. He wrote a bitter editorial in
his newspaper entitled, "A Five Cent Glass of Beer," and from
all over the country funds were sent to him, urging court action
against the bartender.

The success of Fortune as an extraordinary writer attracted
the attention of Amos J. Cummings, publisher of the New York
Evening Sun. He was offered a position as an editorial writer
on the daily, and because of his desire to reach the broadest
possible political sphere of operation, he accepted the position
as an opportunity to aid the Black's cause. It was long after
he joined the staff of the *Evening Sun* that the editor of the
morning daily *Sun* commissioned him to write a series of stories on Haiti. Following the appearance of these articles Fortune was mentioned as the leading candidate to succeed Frederick Douglass as United States Minister to Haiti. But he never
received the appointment, because his political views were in
opposition to the administration. However, Fortune later received from the government a commission to the Philippines.
Upon his return to the United States, he was temporarily out
of the newspaper field. For a time he was a free-lancer.

The *Freeman* was continued under the editorship of Jerome Peters and later its name was changed to the New York *Age*. Peters had as his assistants John Stevens Durham, who had been trained on a Philadelphia daily; Lewis Latimore and Vitorial Mathews. The paper continued to add distinguished writers to its fold. Some of the noted writers were Booker T. Washington, James Weldon Johnson, "Judge" Henry Moore and Josephine Washington. In fact, the *Age* became the first nationally circulated Black newspaper.

Of course, Fortune was not alone in the newspaper field. Some of his correspondents in various sections of the country became publishers and editors of their own newspapers. The more prominent sheets of the period were Christopher J. Perry's Philadelphia *Tribune*, John Mitchell's *Planet*, Harry C. Smith's Cleveland *Gazette*, the Pelhams' Detroit *Plaindealer*, Levi E. Christy's Indianapolis *World*, Calvin Chase's *Washington Bee*, and George L. Knox's Indianapolis *Freeman*.

Chris Perry was born on September 11, 1854 in Baltimore, Maryland, of free parents, and received a limited elementary education before going to Philadelphia. In his new adopted home, Perry availed himself of every educational opportunity offered to him. In 1884 the *Tribune* was first published. Prior to this venture, he had conducted a column of news about Blacks in the (Philadelphia) *Sunday Mercury*. Four years after the journal was launched, Perry wrote,

The Tribune is a paper of the people and for the people. . . . Our past year has been a complete success. We believe that it has been due to our effort to please our patrons and to be worthy of their confidence

Perry clung to the Republican party and resisted appeals to withdraw his support. Unlike Fortune, who advocated an independent position in politics, Perry strongly believed that eventually the desired goal of the Black would come through the Republican party.

Harry Smith was another editor who felt that politics was the means of achieving full citizenship and that the Republican faith had to be upheld. He was born in Clarksburg, West Virginia, January 28, 1863. Two years later he was taken to Cleveland, Ohio, where he received his formal education. His life was occupied with his *Gazette* and politics. He believed that the only way to block a trend toward segregated school systems in Ohio was through united political action. He campaigned for and was elected to the state legislature. His journal then became the "watch dog" of the Republican party against acts placing the Black in an inferior position. When, in 1888, a bill to limit the rights of Blacks was introduced into the Ohio Legislature, Smith wrote in his *Gazette*:

> Sound the alarm! Let the friends of equality for all know that again the enemy seeks to re-enact obnoxious, discriminating and unjust laws. When the time comes, I propose, with the aid of our friends, to oppose it to the death. I write harshly, so that our friends may be aroused through our race advocate, the Gazette.[5]

The *Gazette* was read widely throughout Ohio after Frederick Douglass gave the publisher encouragement. On one occasion, Douglass wrote:

> In the midst of hurried preparation for a long tour in Europe, I snatch my pen, and spend a few moments in telling you how completely I sympathize with you in your political attitude. I do exhort your readers to stand by you in your effort to lead the colored citizens of Ohio to wise political action.[6]

The *Gazette* was not as large in volume as some of the other newspapers. As Smith became more deeply engaged in politics, he used the sheet increasingly as his mouthpiece. His editorial opinion was held in high esteem and he exerted considerable political influence through his paper.

Calvin Chase was born in Washington, February 2, 1854, and his entire life was spent in the nation's capital. He was active in politics, but he was as critical of the Republicans as of the Democrats in his *Washington Bee*. Failure of the National Republican Committee to include an aggressive platform in behalf of Blacks drew scathing attacks in the *Bee*'s editorial

[5]Penn, *Afro-American Press*, p. 283.
[6]*Ibid.*, p. 282.

column. Nor did he spare President Grover Cleveland for not taking more decisive action against the South for ill treatment of Blacks. Under the caption *MURDER AND ASSASSINA-TION,* he wrote,

We are constrained to say that the time has come when murder and the assassination of black Republicans in the South must cease. The time has come for the Negroes and loyal white people of this country to show to the world that there is purity in American politics. In the State of Louisiana, a few days ago, the most cowardly and bloody murders were committed. Innocent colored Republicans were shot down by Democrats like dogs. The same was a repetition of the past brutalities, when helpless colored female virgins and babes were snatched from their beds and murdered. The scene in the South on last Tuesday has raised the indignation of over five million of true black American citizens. It is time for every American Negro in the South to make an appeal to arms and fire every Democratic home where Negro-killers live, from a palace to a hut, in retaliation for the foul and dastardly murders that were committed in the South. We speak without fear and in defense of the helpless Negro. It is far more noble to die the death of a freeman than an ignominious slave. The hundred and fifty-three electoral votes from the South were obtained through theft and assassination; schemes of the most outrageous character were resorted to; Negroes murdered; ballot boxes stuffed; peaceable citizens were imprisoned to prevent them from exercising the rights of elective franchise. Under these circumstances it will cost lives of millions to inaugurate Grover Cleveland.[7]

The reference to Grover Cleveland cost Chase a political appointment.

One newspaperman of the time remarked that Chase kept Washington D.C. literally in a hot blaze. Several years prior to this incident Chase, who favored separate schools for Blacks, had made severe charges about certain members of the school

---

[7]Simmons, p. 129.

board governing the Black school in Washington, and this resulted in some resignations. But more significantly, it caused Douglass to repudiate his friendship with Chase. Years later this difference was patched up.

Chase was strong-willed, but he never matched the daring and courage exemplified by John Mitchell, Jr. and his Richmond *Planet*. Mitchell was born of slave parents on the eve of emancipation and was brought up in his native Virginia. His experiences were similar to those of the majority of Blacks who struggled for survival during the Reconstruction period. He had been one of Fortune's correspondents and took over the editorship of the *Planet* December 5, 1884. Mitchell was not devoted to politics but to what he considered outrages perpetrated against Blacks in his own state. On one occasion a white police officer had shot and fatally wounded a Black. A white jury handed down a verdict that the victim's death was caused by some unknown disease. The case was thoroughly investigated by Mitchell; he followed through every point in the whole case. When his report accused the white policeman of brutal murder, the latter was indicted by the grand jury. The indictment, however, was dropped.

Following a lynching about eight miles from Richmond, Mitchell wrote a vituperative editorial condemning whites for the act. Thereupon, the whites sent a warning that they would hang him if he were to set foot in the county where the lynching took place. Editorially, Mitchell replied,

There are no terrors, Cassius, in your threats, for I am armed so strong in honesty that they pass me by like the idle words, which I respect not.[8]

Furthermore, Mitchell visited the scene and gave a detailed report in the *Planet*. The story literally had the natives standing on their heads, and many white dailies throughout the country either picked up the story or made editorial comment. The old New York *World* commented:

One of the most daring and vigorous Negro editors is John

---

[8]Simmons, p. 319.

Mitchell, Jr., editor of the Richmond *Planet*. The fact that he is a Negro and lives in Richmond does not prevent him from being courageous almost to a fault.[9]

Mitchell had a reporter's sense for running down every lead to a story and he had the courage to print what he observed. He was an important journalist and he practically put a stop to lynching in his state. Besides his success as a journalist Mitchell attained success as a banker. He was the first Negro ever to become a member of the Association of Bankers.

In another section of the country there was another newspaper that was leaning more on enlightenment than on party politics. The Detroit *Plaindealer* was published for the first time, May 19, 1883, by a group that included William H. Anderson, Benjamin B. Pelham, W. H. Stowers, and Robert Pelham, Jr. The *Plaindealer* said that its mission was:

To overcome distrust . . . [to be] an impartial advocate of everything for the welfare of Afro-Americans; to set an example that there is no field of labor which cannot be successfully explored and cultivated by the Afro-American who is energetic and painstaking; to provide a medium for the encouragement of literary work, for the creation of a distinctive and favorable Afro-American sentiment, for the dislodgement of prejudice and for the encouragement of patriotism.[10]

The newspaper had contributors such as Douglass, ex-Senator B. K. Bruce, and ex-Congressman John Lynch, and it was considered one of the leading journals of the period.

Levi Christie's *World* was the first Black newspaper published in the state of Indiana. Founded in Indianapolis in 1884 the paper was continued until about two decades ago. The second Black newspaper to appear was the Indianapolis *Freeman*, first published by Edward E. Cooper. And when Cooper died in 1887, George L. Knox became the publisher and editor. He employed W. Allison Sweeney as his editor, and Sweeney secured a national circulation for the *Freeman*. Later Sweeney

---

[9]New York *World*, February 22, 1887.
[10]Penn, p. 160.

and Knox parted company, and the *Freeman* began to wane. Sweeney for a time worked as contributing editor to the Chicago *Defender*, and then started a paper of his own.

The years beginning around 1880 were a period of new adventure for the Black. And through the newspapers of Fortune's age Booker T. Washington was aided in achieving worldwide fame. In fact—the majority of whites had come to look upon Booker T. Washington as "the leader" of Blacks in America. And in 1915 Washington died, thus marking the end of another significant epoch in Black life.

IX. ACTION ALONG ALL LINES

After Booker T. Washington's death in 1915, not one of his followers or, on the other hand, no one individual who disagreed with his philosophy acquired the position as the sole leader of Blacks in America. The Black no longer rested his case in a singular activity. It was action along all lines—religion, education, business, and organization.

There was a complete rejection of conservative elements that had advocated a more tolerant and persuasive approach in ameliorating discriminatory practices. There was a departure from the traditional adherents of Blacks to the Republican party. The notion prevailed that the major political parties were not different in character, and since they operated for the vested interest of a small economic group, it was wisdom for the Black to split his vote so as to gain greater advantages. The election of 1932 revealed that more Blacks voted Democrat than Republican, which traditionally had been known as the Blacks' party.

The first World War period created a social condition that gave a slight rise in economic opportunities for Blacks, but Woodrow Wilson's slogan "Make The World Safe For Democracy" gave hope that became no more than a myth. The Ku Klux Klan became active again; mob violence was on the rise; suffrage was still denied Blacks in the South; restricted covenants were placed on real estate in the North barring sales to Blacks; and wholesale vandalism took place.

A temporary industrial boom in the North, the toll of the boll weevil, and the "Come North" campaign of Abbott's Chicago *Defender* caused a mass exodus of Blacks from the South. Race riots occurred in various sections. The more serious outbreaks were in East St. Louis, Illinois, Chicago, and Washington, D.C.

During this period, two organizations—one engaged in opening new job opportunities for Blacks in industry and adjusting them to city life and the other devoted to protecting and establishing the constitutional rights of Blacks—took on increased national proportions. They are the National Urban League and the National Association for the Advancement of Colored People.

The National Association for the Advancement of Colored People and the National Urban League did much during this transitional period through their magazines, *The Crisis* and *Opportunity*, to bring about a rebirth of Black art, poetry, and prose. They promoted talented and promising Blacks, including Countee Cullen, Langston Hughes, Effie Lee Newsome, Gwendolyn Bennett, Aaron Douglas, Augusta Savage, and Richmond Barthé.

And not alone did the National Association for the Advancement of Colored People and the Urban League represent the organizational trends among Blacks. The successful organization of a trade union by Blacks showed its first tangible strength in 1929 when the American Federation of Labor granted a charter to the Brotherhood of Sleeping Car Porters.[1] Labor leaders were amazed at the daring courage of a small group of Black Pullman porters, under A. Philip Randolph, who challenged so big a corporation, because the Pullman Company—

. . . has broken every labor union that has ever attempted to organize employees under its jurisdiction. It has broken the biggest strike ever attempted, the Pullman Strike of '93, and we were at a serious disadvantage in attempting to organize

---

[1]The Brotherhood was the first and only Black organization to receive an international charter from the AFL. There are 52 locals for Pullman porters, 14 locals for train porters, and 12 locals for locomotive firemen.

against such a corporation unless we were a part of the organized labor movement of America. As a result of that effort we sought affiliation with the American Federation of Labor.[2]

Randolph's adult life had been devoted to unpopular causes. He had been an ardent crusader in demanding respect for the common worker. He was born in Crescent City, Fla., in 1889. His father was a Methodist minister. He received his early educational training at the Cookman Institute, Jacksonville, Fla., which became widely known after its merger with Mrs. Mary McLeod Bethune's school at Daytona Beach. His formal training was supplemented at City College of New York and his education enriched by constant reading.

Prior to his significant leadership of the March-on-Washington Movement, Randolph had achieved his greatest undertaking—the organization of Pullman porters. That was not his first effort in organizing workers. He had many years earlier attempted to organize apartment building custodians. He lectured all over the country on economic affairs that hampered the advancement of Blacks. He had campaigned for the offices as assemblyman, secretary of the state of New York and congressman on the Socialist party's ticket. He had been co-editor of *The Messenger* magazine with Chandler Owen. He had been thrown in jail during World War I because he was a conscientious objector and urged other Negroes not to fight since America did not include them in her "creed." In every thing he attempted, there was almost certain failure because of the forces operating against progressive movement. In spite of all the setbacks, eventually Randolph was successful in making the most significant contribution to the economic well being of Blacks in America.

This is the civilization in which the Black press had to function as the oracle of Black folk. It was only about thirty years after Reconstruction that a Hampton (Virginia) Institute graduate launched an insignificant looking newspaper in Chicago.

---

[2]Report of Proceedings of Biennial Convention and 15th Anniversary Celebration of the Brotherhood of Sleeping Car Porters, New York City, S 15-20, 1940, p. 18.

Those who observed the first issues of the paper thought of the editor's effort as merely a joke. And ten years later the editor, Robert Stengstacke Abbott, was known all over the country because of his Chicago *Defender*.

He went to Chicago in 1896 from Hampton Institute, where he had trained as a printer. Besides his regular school work, Abbott had been a member of the school's quartet, singing tenor. This extracurricular activity had given him an opportunity to travel about the country and hear talks by prominent Blacks. Among these were Frederick Douglass and Ida B. Wells, whose newspaper was destroyed by a white mob in Memphis, Tennessee.

Both persons made deep impressions and inspired him to dream of running a newspaper. Before going to Hampton, Abbott had attended the secondary school which was a part of Claffin University. He had gone there from his native home in Savannah, Georgia, where he had worked as a printer's apprentice on the *Savannah* (daily) *News*.

Upon arriving in Chicago, Abbott tried to secure a job in a well-regulated printing establishment. Failing in his search he took odd jobs. During the time he was working at jobs, he attended the evening classes at Kent Law School and was graduated from that institution. Later he went into business for himself. He was befriended by being given the free use of a basement in an apartment house on the South Side. Abbott's complete equipment consisted of a bottle of paste, a pair of scissors, a couple of soap boxes, and a kitchen table. That was the *Defender* in 1909.

Abbott did everything himself—the printing, writing, soliciting of advertisements, and the selling of the newspapers. His articles were sentimental and accounts of personal happenings. As the *Defender* developed as a militant crusader against lynching and discrimination, the editor never lost his touch for a good human interest story. Two investigators recently revealed:

Though Abbott continued for sometime as a sole regular staff member, he enlisted a number of volunteers. Julius N. Avendorph, sports promoter and social figure, wrote about both fields of interest. Tony Langston, a bartender at the

Keepstone Club, took advantage of his position to gather news about frequenters of the establishment—Alfred Anderson, manager of Old Provident Hospital, helped out with editorials, and Dr. A. Wilberforce Williams edited a health column.[3]

One of the first full-time newspapermen to join the *Defender* staff was J. Hockley Smiley, son of a Philadelphia caterer. Smiley had a real newspaper flare. He had attempted the publishing of his own journal and failed. Then he went to the *Defender* and began organizing promotional plans for circulation. By 1915 the newspaper was developing into one of the biggest newspaper ventures ever successfully operated by a Black; and the slogan "World's Greatest Weekly" was adopted for it by the publisher.

Abbott was the first Black publisher to adopt the typographical style of the present-day daily newspapers. He imitated the typographical style of the sensational Hearst newspapers of 1912 and gave his sheet every appearance of the metropolitan journals. Big headline type, red ink, news stories of the kind to attract attention made the *Defender* sell, and in 1928 its circulation was reported as being over half a million, with readers in many foreign countries.

The *Defender* was big business. The newspaper's plant was equipped with modern machinery for producing a newspaper like any of the largest daily newspapers. First-class mechanics and union-certified master printers were hired to operate the plant. In the early twenties there were very few Blacks who were members of the printing craft union, so the mechanical staff was manned completely by whites. However, Abbott prevailed upon the local union to take in Black apprentices.

The *Defender's* editorial policy was clear-cut. Abbott wanted the Black to share everything on the same basis as whites. He was opposed to segregation and discrimination on account of race or color. That policy was followed on all scores. For instance, an article appearing in the October 22, 1947 issue read:

---

[3]Anna Bontemps and Jack Conroy, *They Seek a City* (New York: Doubleday, Doran Co., Inc., 1945), pp. 83-84.

Prisoners Segregated From Bomb Outrages

Bomb outrages that endanger life and property are indications that maniacs are at large in this city. The police after apprehending these bombers, who are in most cases, foreigners not far removed from the semicircularized regions of Europe, put them in well-kept cells. In contrast to this treatment of these radical violators of law and order, Race men arrested on minor charges are confined in ill-kept, segregated cell blocks, away from other prisoners, as if they were afflicted with a plague. The white prisoners who are subjected to insanity tests are handled with velvet gloves and even allowed to eat before Race prisoners are served, so that the two groups will not come in contact with each other. The prison officials state that this method is used to prevent race disturbances. If this is true why aren't there hundreds of riots in progress throughout the city wherever members of the two races come in contact?

The real reason is that these bigoted minds are enforcing rules of racial intolerance. The citizens can crush this propaganda of hatred by demanding all rights of citizenship. If these rights are denied by the restaurant owners, storekeepers, and theaters, go into the courts and fight the breeders of intolerance with the civil rights law of Illinois. Demand and get every consideration in all walks of life. They are given the foreigners who do not even enjoy the rights of citizenship and American birth.

Abbot was also sensitive to community problems and obstacles that Blacks faced. He constantly called attention to a situation such as:

More Policewomen Are Needed to Meet Call

A lone woman shoulders the heavy responsibility of interpreting the problem of Race girls who are being apprehended daily. The burden is becoming a perplexing problem with the increase of delinquent girls. During the past several years there has been a big influx of girls coming here from the South with hopes of bettering their conditions. By being

112

lured into bad company they fall into the hands of the authorities. One Race woman out of 35 women of the police department has devoted her energies to investigating and trying to find some immediate remedy for the wayward girl. This work is needed and must be done by more Race policewomen. We must have more policewomen.

As an illustration of his campaign to instill social responsibility in the community, the following item appeared in the October 27, 1927 issue of the *Defender*:

Beautify Cemeteries

There is nothing more desolate in appearance than a neglected cemetery. Among the most forsaken-looking are the ones in which our people are buried in the majority. After the funeral is over the graves should not be forgotten. Undertakers should devise some plans for securing perpetual care in cemeteries. This sort of upkeep should follow as a matter of pride.

He believed in intermarriage and complete assimilation. He wanted full equality for the Black. He wanted the Black to develop race pride and not race consciousness. He urged them to become educated to fit into his community as useful citizens. The *Defender's* platform was set forth to erase racial barriers and place the Black in the mainstream of American democracy. Under the masthead of the newspaper on the editorial page in each issue was printed this platform for America:

1. The opening up of all trades and trade unions to Blacks as well as whites.
2. The appointment of a member of the Race to the president's cabinet.
3. Men of our Race in police departments over entire United States.
4. Engineers and firemen of our Race on all American railroads, steamships, and government-controlled industries.
5. Government schools open to all American citizens in preference to foreigners.

6. Motormen and conductors of our Race on street railways throughout the United States.

To Abbott, those were vital issues that had to be solved if Blacks were to advance toward full citizenship. They were moral issues, for the publisher believed as expressed editorially January 21, 1928:

American citizenship means nothing if it does not carry with it the right to be men and women in every sense of the words. If it does not insure protection against discrimination and injustices, against peonage and slavery, against concubinage and mobbery, it means less than nothing.

But these are rights we must demand and insist upon. Any person has the right to exercise all of these evils against the man or woman who will accept them! And for 60 years we have accepted them, although our constitution—ours by right of heritage and sacrifice—has provided protection against them.

We must demand! Where we are not granted them, we also accept that as our lot. This must stop. If we are to be accorded the rights that are ours, we must show a determination to have them.

Let us begin now to be Americans—real Americans!

In every edition of the paper were to appear especially prepared articles urging Blacks to do specific things, such as to improve themselves or to act on important issues. Every worker on the staff from the copy boy to the general manager knew that stories known as "R.S.A. Must" took priority over every other article in the newspaper and had to be given space. And there were no slip-ups. The stories told of the advantages to the Black in knowing foreign languages, skilled trades, and in saving his earnings. He advocated the free intermingling of mixed couples and admonished Blacks not to act shy or avoid being seen in public if they were married to white persons. He crusaded for the erection of a monument in honor of the 15th Regiment, which fought in World War I. The memorial now stands at 35th Street and South Parkway (Chicago). Special campaign appeals for charity and relief funds were often added to this list.

In directing the editorial policy of the *Defender*, one of Abbott's most exacting rules set down for his staff to follow was to avoid designating Blacks as "Blacks" or "colored." If it were absolutely necessary to distinguish between Blacks and whites, Blacks were referred to as "the Race," with a capital "R". Abbott wanted to avoid any words that created the impression in the minds of his readers that Blacks were inferior.

Around 1918 the *Defender* was recognized by the white leaders as an influential journal among Blacks. Political leaders in both houses of Congress read into their records articles and editorials that were printed in the *Defender*. Perhaps its greatest influence was demonstrated when it is said to have started an exodus of Blacks from the South during and after World War I. This wave of migration caused a swelling of population on Chicago's South Side. And the newspaper was accused of precipitating the Chicago riots in 1919. The newspaper plant in which the *Defender* was being printed at this time refused to print it fearing mob violence. This led Abbott to make plans for establishing a complete plant for handling his paper. In various sections of the South the paper was barred from newsstands, and sales on the street were prohibited.

Southern dailies quite often carried vituperative editorials about the *Defender*. Almost any subject would be seized upon by many of the southern journals endeavoring to diminish the *Defender*'s influence. An example of a tirade by the Jackson (Mississippi) *Daily News* was reprinted in the January 21, 1928 issue of the *Defender*:

The Chicago Defender is a Negro Newspaper published in the Windy City, apparently for the special delectation of the almost whites and high-yallers among the Negroes of that community.

* * * *

Apparently the publication is prosperous, for its advertising pages are well filled, chiefly with advertisements proclaiming the merits of various hair-straightening remedies.

Long ago the Colored folks in the South found out that there never was, and never will be, a remedy that will permanently take the kink out of a Negro's hair.

However, that discovery has apparently not reached the 200,000 or more Negroes in Chicago—and therefore, the advertising department of "The Chicago Defender" is apparently prosperous.

* * * *

A recent issue of "The Chicago Defender," sent to the *Daily News* by special delivery, contains the following editorial:

> In his campaign speech, just prior to his election as governor of Mississippi, Brother Bilbo, according to 'The World Tomorrow' made the following statement: 'There are not 2,000 Negroes qualified to vote.' 'The World Tomorrow' follows this up with the statement that 'The United States census of 1920 declares that of 453,663 Negroes 21 years of age and over living in Mississippi 290,282 can read and write.'
>
> With these facts upon which to work, the question now is, how did governor Bilbo get elected? . . . Just what, besides being white, is a qualification to vote in Mississippi?
>
> And, incidentally, wasn't it this same governor Bilbo, who, during one of his previous administrations, wired Dr. DuBois in answer to a query as to what he intended to do about a lynching in that state: 'Nothing, go to h---!' " was his reply.

Abbott himself took an active leadership in community affairs. He purchased a palatial home on South Parkway. He was a patron of the arts, including the Chicago Civic Opera Company. He traveled through South America. And the newspaper accounts of his activity always were angled to encourage others to broaden their activities as citizens.

Black newspapers were criticized severely for not assuming a role of leadership in the light of social change. In February 1922, the *Messenger* proclaimed:

116

The march of Negro radical and liberal thought may be slow, but it is sure. That the masses of the Negroes will awake to the fact that they are being betrayed by their leaders to their enemies is as sure as the night follows the day.

... our only hope lies in a militant, uncompromising aggressive, intelligent, New Negro—a Negro whose ideals are unpurchasable and who subordinates his own personal interests to the interests of the masses.

The radicals regarded the period as calling for dynamic leadership in the economic field and, in their opinion, the Black press was ignorant. Many of the newspapers like the New York *Amsterdam News* under the editorship of William M. Kelly, and Chester Franklin's Kansas City *Call*, Robert L. Vann's *Pittsburgh Courier*, Fred Moore's *New York Age*, the Murphy's *Afro-American*, Roscoe Diengee's *Black Dispatch*, the *Chicago Bee, Dallas Express, Washington American, Portland Advocate, and Pacific Defender* (not so widely known as the Chicago *Defender*) gave space to opinions expressed by the radical group.

Thus it is quite understandable that when the Pullman Company endeavored to block the independent organization of the porters, the Black newspapers were attacked for failing to openly support the porters' union. Because of the Chicago *Defender's* large circulation that newspaper was important.

Reluctance or refusal of any newspaper to support union effort of the Pullman porters was regarded as a policy of compromise. Thus the *Messenger* in this editorial called upon Abbott to declare himself.

X. SPEAK UP, MR. ABBOTT

The *World's Greatest Weekly* has been weighed in the balance and found wanting. The movement to organize the Pullman porters was the straw that broke the camel's back.

The *Chicago Defender* has thrown its weight on the side of the Pullman Company and against the Pullman porters by giving space to the propaganda of the company and denying the porters a hearing.

117

According to many porters, the circulation of the *Defender* was largely built up by porters carrying bundles around the country, getting agents for it. The paper owes much of its power to the porters and now it turns against them.

Does Abbott need the money the Pullman Company is giving for its opposition to the Brotherhood? Hardly. He has gotten along without it so far. It is obvious to every intelligent person that if the Brotherhood fails or succeeds, the black papers that have sold out, will receive no more Pullman money. They have never before received any support from the Pullman Company, but they have from the porters. Enlightened self interest ought to dictate their supporting their race movements.

Now the *Defender*, the *Whip*, the *Argus*, etc., are stacked up by the thousands in the offices of the Company, and the porters are religiously urged and persuaded to take copies. Why is the Pullman Company so interested in the porters reading Negro papers now? Simply because the *Defender* and some others are opposing the struggle of the men for a living wage. Before this, if Brother Abbott had walked into a Pullman Office and began handing out copies of the *Defender* to the porters, the officials would have either kicked him out or had him impounded in some asylum for insanity. But now he is needed to help them chloroform the porters.

As a newspaperman, Mr. Abbott is obliged to give space to both sides of a controversy involving such big and vital questions as this movement. No white paper in the country, has taken such a palpably unfair position as the *Defender* has. The *Chicago Daily News*, *The New York Times*, *World*, *Journal*, *Sun* and *Globe*, *St. Louis Post Dispatch*, *Omaha Bee*, and numerous others, have carried splendid reports of the Brotherhood, and all favorable, too. Note too, that these are white papers that do not depend upon Blacks buying them for their existence, whereas, the *Defender* and black papers, in general, do entirely upon black patrons, and still, Abbott carries lurid headlines, misrepresentations and malicious lies against the Brotherhood for the Company and not a line for the porters. This is well nigh inconceivable. But miracles may happen with black leaders under the pressure of money.

We still feel that Brother Abbott's heart is all right, though it is apparent that his head is wrong, or his hands are tied.

The only reason which can be assigned for his attitude is that he is a director of the Binga State Bank, and the Pullman Porters Benefit Association has ten thousand dollars on deposit there. This Association, of course, is controlled by the Pullman Company which would compel it to withdraw its deposits, should Abbott, a director, carry in the *Defender*, anything in the interest of the porters' organization. This undoubtedly is the real reason.

But Abbott should have had guts enough to say to the Pullman Company, I'll carry any legitimate advertising; but I'll not carry your propaganda as news unless I give the same opportunity to the porters. This would have been fair, manly, honest. True he has not carried an editorial against the porters but the news propaganda is far more effective than editorials.

This presents a very serious situation to the race. Our biggest weekly permits itself to be gagged by a rich corporation in order to retain a $10,000 deposit in the Binga Bank, from which Mr. Abbott profits. Mr. Abbott speak up, is it true or not true? Are ten thousand dollars more important to the race than the lives of 12,000 porters and their families?[1]

The strong position held by the newspaper was seriously threatened in 1926 when the *Defender* failed to take up the fight of the Pullman porters. The porters had the support of the *Messenger*, a monthly magazine founded in 1917 with Chandler Owen and A. Philip Randolph as co-editors. The editors and their associates were known as radicals because of their militancy and their severe criticism of Black leaders. Among the writers were Robert W. Bagnall, Myra H. Colson, Abraham L. Harris, Theophilus Lewis, Ernest Rice McKinney, William Pickens, Sr., J. A. Rogers, George S. Schuyler, and Lovett Fort-Whiteman. Editorially the *Messenger* had inaugurated the period of the New Negro in May 1919 when it made this declaration:

---

[1]Editorial, "Speak up Mr. Abbott," *The Messenger Magazine,* January 26, pp. 16-17.

A New Crowd—A New Negro

Throughout the world among all peoples and classes, the clock of social progress is striking the high noon of the Old Crowd, and why?

The Old Crowd enjoins the Negro to be conservative, when he has nothing to conserve. Neither his life nor his property receives the protection of the government which conscripts his life to "make the world safe for democracy". The conservative in all lands are the wealthy and the ruling class. The Negro is in dire poverty and he is not part of the ruling class.

In the Negro schools and colleges . . . [the leaders are] reactionary. In the press . . . [the editors]—are compromising. In politics . . . me-too-boss gang of Negro Republican politicians are hopelessly ignorant and distressingly unwitting of their way.

In Church the Old Crowd still preaches that "the meek will inherit the earth" . . . and "You may take all this world but give me Jesus" . . . constitute the subjects of the Old Crowd, for black men and women who are overworked and underpaid, lynched, Jim-Crowed and disfranchised—a people who are not yet languishing in the dungeons of ignorance and superstition.

As among all other peoples, the New Crowd must be composed of young men who are educated, radical and fearless . . . the conditions for joining the New Crowd are: ability, radicalism and sincerity . . . the New Crowd is uncompromising. Its tactics are not defensive but offensive. It would not send notes after a Negro is lynched. It would not appeal to white leaders. It would appeal to the plain working people everywhere. The New Crowd sees that the war came, that the Negro fought, bled and died; that the war has ended, and he is not free.

The New Crowd would have no armistice with lynch-law; no truce with Jim-Crowism, and disfranchisement; no peace until the Negro receives complete social, economic and political justice.

About twelve months later the *Defender* declared itself for

120

the Pullman porters' union and began printing releases favorable to their organization. But the *Defender* never regained its former undisputed position of leadership.

Although the publisher lived until 1940, the age of Abbott ended around 1932, when he became ill and less active in the management of the *Defender*. The newspaper is now directed by Abbott's nephew, John Stengstacke.

The organizing of Pullman porters into an independent union was a mean and difficult job. Leaders of the movement met stiff resistance from every quarter, and the porters themselves were threatened with the loss of their jobs if they formed the union. Available places for the porters to hold meetings were few and often spies were said to be revealing their plans to the Pullman Company.

Thus the Black newspapers were an important medium for the porters' movement. And when, as in the case of the Chicago *Defender*, the newspaper did not take a position in favor of the union, the porters boycotted the publication. Nevertheless they did not criticize the newspapers until the papers accepted paid advertisements from the Pullman Company and refused to carry reports released by the union. A direct attack on the porters' movement by the Chicago *Whip* caused Randolph and Owen to retaliate. And no other Black newspaper has ever been subjected to such a campaign as the one carried on against the *Whip*, eventually causing the publication to go out of business.

The union organizer Randolph took up the fight after the *Whip* in their October 15, 1925 issue referred to the union idea as built on quicksand. The paper also said that the American Federation of Labor was flirting with the porters. Randolph labeled the assertion bluntly—a lie. He further replied in the December 1925 issue of the *Messenger* that:

The American Federation of Labor, as is proper and natural, is lending its moral support to the movement to organize the porters, which every Negro ought to welcome and be proud of. . . . Is it a crime to enlist five million organized white workers on the porters' side in the fight for a living wage? Certainly not. In one breath, like a child, you are crying because the American Federation of Labor, as you claim, is denying Negro workers entrance into the Unions, and, in the next breath, you throw up your hands in holy horror because some Negro workers are intelligent enough to accept the hand of white workers when extended to them. . . .

. . . You are not opposing the Brotherhood of Sleeping-Car Porters because you think it is connected with the American Federation of Labor. That is merely an excuse, not the reason. You had to hunt for a convenient excuse to justify your unreasonable and foolish attack on the most vitally constructive, economic movement ever begun by Negroes in America. The real reason is the advertising you are getting from the Pullman Company to oppose the movement. . . .

Randolph, gifted in coining apt slogans, called the *Whip* the "Chicago Flip" and referred to its editor, Joseph D. Bibbs, as "Joe D. Blibbs, idiot-or."

In the *Messenger* one month later, Chandler Owen who had then become editor of the Chicago *Bee*, began his series entitled "The Neglected Truth."

For about six years colored Chicago has been bedeviled by a small irresponsible publication edited by a man whose presumption is exceeded only by his ignorance. Publications must live off circulation and advertising, and circulation usually comes from interesting news matter presented to one's readers. The Chicago *Whip* could command neither circulation nor advertising, so it thought out and presented a new policy on Negro newspaperdom; it inaugurated blackmail. . . .

That was a part of the introduction to an exposé of alleged graft, blackmail, and a "shake-down," practiced by Bibb, the editor, and A.C. McNeal, the publisher. Owen gave names of gambling places and vice dens, quoting the names of their operators and amounts of money paid to the *Whip* as "hush money" for their threats to print stories unfavorable to the illegal businesses.

Owen said there was only one exception to the *Whip*'s "shake-down" racket. This was in the case of three houses that were attacked and:

The owner was said to have been Al Capone, alias Al Brown, notorious Cicero, Illinois gangster and bootlegger . . . These places were attacked on several occasions, but Capone refused to give Bibb and the *Whip* any money. Instead, he threatened the lives of the publishers.

Of the most daring charges, Owen accused the *Whip* not only of wrecking one of the largest old-line insurance companies operated by Blacks, but also of causing a bank to fail, and of causing the death of Frank Gillespie, president of another large insurance company.

In the third article of the series, Owen's "The Neglected Truth" told how the utility interests were using Bibb, McNeal, and the *Whip*. The deal was a deliberate effort, he observed, to bulldoze and control Black opinion. And he wrote:

There is just now being formed in Chicago a National Negro Advertising Agency. The object and purpose are to organize the various public utility interests of the different cities where colored papers are published, and to amass a fund from these utility interests with a view to controlling and shaping colored opinion by the giving of advertising. . . .

In the white man's mind for some time, the idea was shunted on its course with accelerated speed through the organization of the Brotherhood of Sleeping Car Porters. During this fight, which is just starting, despite the wholesale buying up of many Negro papers, there were certain ones, like the *Pittsburgh Courier*, the *New York Age*, the Baltimore *Afro-American*, the Chicago *Bee*, the Washington *Tribune*, the Kansas City *Call* and others which would not bend supple hinges on the knee to the God of Baal. Some of these papers received advertising, as they had a right to do, but insisted that advertisers did not buy their editorial columns.

The *Whip* brought court action against Owen and Randolph. When trial was called, the case was dismissed in short order. The Pullman porters had won their first big moral victory.

A "Back to Africa" movement also came and went like a comet during this period. It was the wild dream of Marcus

Garvey. And the *Negro World*, Garvey's mouthpiece, was but one of his fantastic enterprises. Garvey was born in the year 1887 at St. Anne's Parish, Jamaica, British West Indies. Following his elementary training in the public schools, he was sent by his parents to a private institution. Later he learned some skill as a printer. As a young man he went to England and attended for a time one of the universities. While in London, Garvey's dream of setting up a strong Black kingdom formed in his mind. After twice working his way on a cattle boat across the ocean to America, he decided that the United States was the place to inaugurate his plan.

Garvey was a forceful speaker, and with dramatic stunts dazzled and entertained his audiences. This was his appeal:

> We have reached the time when every minute, every second must count for something done, something achieved in the cause of Africa. We need the freedom of Africa now. At this moment methinks I see Ethiopia stretching forth her bonds unto God, the Race, the Black, and the Green, and saying: 'Men of the Negro race, men of Ethiopia, follow me!"[1]

The *Negro World* echoed Garvey's appeal. The sheet started as a daily and the editorial staff consisted chiefly of young newspapermen he had brought from England. Perhaps it was because their slant on running a newspaper was so different from the general American style that the sheet became a huge financial loss. The daily eventually was suspended and the *Negro World* was continued as a weekly. The very distinguished journalist of the last generation, Fortune, approaching the last of a long, active career, became the editor. Whatever fine talents Fortune possessed as a writer or editor were dimmed by the flamboyant Garvey. The entire front page was devoted to "A Message from Marcus Garvey." The messages bore captions such as these:

Africa Must Be Free
Africa Our Salvation
Africa—A Nation, One and Indivisible

---

[1]Mary White Ovington, *Portraits in Color* (New York: Viking Press, 1927), p. 18.

Garvey's organization for sponsoring his "Back to Africa" movement was known as the Universal Improvement Association, Inc. Titles accorded to the officials of the organization sounded as though they were already a part of a reigning dynasty in Africa. Of course Garvey was His Excellency, the Provisional President of Africa. His subordinates were Knight Commanders of the Distinguished Order of Ethiopia and Knight Commanders of the Sublime Order of the Nile. The underlings had varying titles and ranks in the make-believe African Army. The women made up the Black Cross Nurses.

Garvey and his active staff wore elaborate uniforms, patterned after those of the Knights of Columbus and the Masons. The army leaders wore snappy uniforms on the style of the United States Army, but with drab green breeches, black shirts, and red trim. The flag was black, green, and red.

To subsidize the establishment of the Black Republic, Garvey made appeals for the contribution of funds; and to capture the Negro's imagination and membership, he bought four useless, obsolete steamships and through his newspaper shouted about the Black Star Lines. He operated a group of small hand laundries in Harlem, a group of neighborhood bakeries, and a few factories. And he got as far as the basement in the erection of Liberty Hall—what was to have been the mecca of Black folk of the world. Garvey's impractical scheme was ended by the Ku Klux Klan in order to thrust the Negro into a coma and distract him from more fundamental issues.

Unfortunately, Garvey was shot in 1919 by a crank and he instantly became a hero of Black drama. The white dailies in New York City began giving his night parades and speeches unlimited space, and the *Negro World* soon boasted of the U.N.I.A.'s one-million membership. Local offices were established in practically every large city in the country.

The general Black press was cool to the Garvey publication and it was often said that the Black newspapers fought him bitterly with their indifference. Editorially the *New York Age* made this prophecy:

Despite all of Marcus Garvey's protestations, despite even the faith which he may have in himself, his ventures are found to impress many as neither realistic nor sound. They are not commerce undiluted. They are not combined policies. Nor are they passionately devoted to the idea undefiled. They are a dangerous merger of all elements, most dangerous of all for Mr. Garvey, and for those individuals who are moved to give their confidence and their funds. The bill has not yet been presented to Mr. Garvey. It may be a heavy one on the day of payment.

The radicals went directly after Garvey and his movement. The following editorial in the September 1921 *Messenger* analyzed the situation:

Garveyism

Garveyism is an upshot of the Great World War. It sprang forth amidst the wild currents of national, racial and class hatreds and prejudices stirred and unleashed by the furious flames of battle. Under the strains and stresses of conflict, the state power and institutions of the ruling peoples were mobilized.

The fallacy . . . consists in its total disregard of the relative malice of the thing proposed to those for whom it is proposed. . . . Certainly, an intelligent person would not advocate an admittedly unscientific and inefficient plan of action in industry, business or finance, on the highly questionable grounds, that Negroes should have such an enterprise of their own for their own. For, palpably, no benefits can flow to a people from the adoption of a program which the collective intelligence of society has discarded.

The shipping business is controlled by a Shipping Trust.

It is about as possible and necessary to maintain a fleet of ships for Negroes only, as it is to build and maintain a railroad alongside that of the Pennsylvania Railroad for Negroes only.

The very fact that the great European powers have fought to conquer Africa, is pretty good evidence that they don't intend surrendering it to the cry of "Africa for Africans." Thus, it means war to the death against formidable armies and navies of single fighting craft.

December 10, 1921, pp. 26-27.

The whites in America don't take Garveyism seriously. They dub Garvey a "Moses of the Negro" in order to get Negroes to follow him, which will wean them away from any truly radical economic program. They know that the achievement of his program, the redemption of Africa is unattainable, but it serves the purpose of engaging the Negroes' brains, energy and funds in a highly nebulous, futile and doubtful movement so far as beneficial results to Negroes are concerned.

. . . In very truth, a striking anti-white-man doctrine is both unsound and dangerous. For it is false to assume that all white men are agreed upon a program of opposition to Negroes. Garveyism is spiritual; the need now, however, is a Negro renaissance in scientific thought.

There was no letup by the *Messenger* in their attacks on Garvey. From the South came threats because of the aggressive campaign. For instance, the *Messenger*, October 1922, reported in its own columns:

The Human Hand Threat

On Tuesday afternoon . . . September 5, while sitting in my office, I received a package marked "from a friend." This anonymous sender forthwith aroused my suspicions. . . . I noticed a whitish powder falling out of it. This confirmed my suspicions of there being some foul play intended. Hence . . . I telephoned the . . . police . . . posthaste, they came over to my office . . . and placed it in water to prevent an explosion in the event that its contents were explosive material.

To the utter amazement and horror of everyone, upon opening the package a human hand was found. In the box also this letter:

"Listen Randolph
"We have been watching your writings in all your papers for quite a while but we want you to understand before we

act. If you are not in favor with your own race movement you can't be with ours. There is no space in our race for you and your creed. What do you mean by giving us a nigger? Do you know that our organization is made up of all whites?

"We have sent you a sample of our good work, so watch your step or else you . . .

Now let me see your name in your nigger improvement association as a member, paid up too, in about one week from now. Don't worry about lynching in the South. If you were here you wouldn't talk about it. Now be careful how you publish this letter in your magazine or we may have to send your hand to someone else.

"Don't think we can't get you and your crowd. Although you are in New York City it is just as easy as if you were in Georgia. If you can't unite with your own race we will find out what's the matter with you all. Don't be selfish. Give your friends a tip.   KKK"

Their reasons given were: 1) the bitter hatred of the Klan for the position of the *Messenger* and its editors on "social equality," economic and political. This position had been, time and again, buttressed up by the most exhaustive writing and platform propaganda from coast to coast. For quite some years the *Messenger* editors have been directing a systematic and vigorous campaign through the large white unions against the Klan.

Still the work against treacherous, unscrupulous, disloyal Negro leaders as well as against the Klan will go unabated. With redoubled efforts, I shall mobilize all of my energies in order to destroy black and white Ku Kluxism in America.

As evidence of this resolve, the Sunday following the receiving of the hand, I assailed Marcus Garvey and the KKK more violently than ever before, and it was hailed by the largest audience yet assembled which applauded more vociferously than ever before.

Thus the slogan under which this crusade began—*Marcus Garvey Must Go!*—will be reinforced with "and the Ku Klux Klan too."

Garvey was later convicted of using the mails to defraud

with the role of stock in the Black Star Line, Inc. and sentenced to the Federal Prison at Atlanta, Ga. on February 8, 1925, and, although he continued his messages in the *Negro World*, it was the end of the "Back to Africa" movement.

Black migration from the South to the North sharpened the competition with whites for jobs and housing. Whites resorted to discrimination and segregation patterns. The Black leaders had hoped for relief through President Wilson, who promised to abolish such practices in government and the armed services. If anything, the segregation pattern became more entrenched during his second administration.

The president was bitterly assailed by Monroe Trotter of the Boston *Guardian*. Trotter attracted national attention in an open letter of castigation addressed to President Wilson for failing to keep his promise of eliminating segregation in the armed services and departments of government. In a personal conference with the president, Trotter provoked Wilson's animosity because he resented the chief executive's lecture as though he were a student. Wilson never stopped acting like a schoolteacher.

Trotter continued his fight for the equal rights of Blacks. In Boston, the *Guardian* never ceased its campaign to block the establishment of segregated branches of the Young Men's and Women's Christian Association. A letter appearing in the editorial columns of the newspaper reflected the paper's policy:

I am a Bostonian. Boston is the city of my birth. Here have I lived and breathed on the air of liberty and enjoyment of privileges freely offered alike to white and colored. In all my varied experiences in Boston I have yet to recognize the need of separate educational institutions—separate YMCA's.

In an editorial, Trotter's determined position against segregation is expressed:

Peonage, disfranchisement, lynching are the grosser evils. Any grade of people would object to them. Our race shows its quality in so far as it resents civil displacements, disabilities and discriminations. These things are badges of inferiority of status and chief test of these is every form of civic segregation. . . . Refuse to be a party to segregation in the free North and you raise your grade among the races of the world. Stand fast for equality of status.[1]

Every Black newspaper was opposed to segregation, and the celebrated Sweet case of Detroit was an occasion for the press to rally the whole Black population against its insidious practice by whites.

The Sweet case broke on September 8, 1925, when Dr. Ossian H. Sweet, a Black physician of Detroit, moved into a house he had purchased in a white neighborhood. On the following day a white mob congregated around the dwelling located on the corner of Garland Street and Charlevoix Avenue with the preconceived plan to drive the newcomer out of the neighborhood.

In the home when the mob attacked were, besides Dr. and Mrs. Sweet, his brother, Dr. O.O. Sweet, a dentist; Henry Sweet, a college senior; a classmate of Henry's, John Latting; a personal friend, William Davis, a federal narcotics officer; and the physician's chauffeur, Joe Mack. But the Sweets were supplied with ammunition, and a white man, Leo Breiner, was killed. Dr. Sweet later told an all white jury sitting in Judge Frank Murphy's courtroom with his family and friends as defendants on a charge of murder:

When I opened the door and saw the mob, I realized I was facing the same mob that had hounded my people through its entire history. In my mind I was pretty confident of what I was up against. I had my back against the wall. I was filled with a peculiar fear, the fear of one who knows the history of my race. I knew what that mob had done to my people before.[2]

This charge was more than a specific testimony of a physician, his family and friends. It was a declaration of the Black race against segregation. The NAACP under the guidance of

---

[1]Frederick G. Detweiler, *Negro Press in the United States* (Chicago: Chicago Press, 1922).

[2]Arthur Garfield Hayes, *Let Freedom Ring* (New York: Boni and Liveright, 1928), p. 226.

James Weldon Johnson, executive secretary, and Walter White, assistant secretary, undertook the responsibility of providing the outstanding criminal lawyer of the country, Clarence Darrow, and a staff of lawyers including Arthur Garfield Hayes, Julian Perry, Rowlette and Mahoney, Walter Nelson, and Herman K. Friedman.

Through the support of the Black newspapers over the cost for the defense originally estimated at $50,000 was raised. And the *Age*, the (Baltimore) *Afro-American*, the *Pittsburgh Courier*, the *Defender*, the *Black Dispatch*, the (California) *Eagle*, the (Kansas City) *Call*, the (Cleveland) *Call*, the Dallas *Express*, the (Dayton) *Forum*, the (Detroit) *Independent*, the (Florida) *Sentinel*, the *Houston Informer*, the (Indianapolis) *Recorder*, the (Norfolk) *Journal and Guide*, the (Louisville) *Leader*, the (Omaha) *Guide*, the (St. Louis) *Argus*, the (Savannah) *Independent*, and the (Cincinnati) *Union* were among those newspapers giving unlimited space in the fight for "freedom of residence." The defendants in the Sweet case were acquitted nearly two years later, but the fight against segregation was still being waged by the Black newspapers.

With the coming of the economic depression (1929) discrimination against and segregation of Blacks was on the rise. And the problem became more complex for the Black newspapers, for there were still many things undone: particularly in the South blacks were unable to vote, they had only limited employment opportunities, they were denied full protection of the law and fair trial by law in courts, they had inadequate schools and dilapidated houses in which to dwell.

XI. A FEELING OF CITIZENSHIP

During the depression years, Blacks suffered more, on the whole, than any other group because of their basically lower economic level. Their lot was improved somewhat with the New Deal Administration because of federal social legislation. The new political regime created for the Black a psychological feeling of citizenship. And perhaps more gains were made by the Black toward citizenship during the first eight years of this administration than in the whole period from 1880 to 1932.

In the New Deal Administration a Black leadership, commonly called the "black cabinet," was developed, as in practically every department and agency of the government a Black held either an advisory position or a post as director of Black affairs.

Agitation on the part of the Black press at the beginning of the New Deal had a lot to do with this innovation in government. There were other factors. There was the "brain trust" era, which made a serious effort to find actual facts about social conditions, and the black expert was sought for firsthand information. There was the Rosenwald Fund, which had provided a Black adviser on economic affairs in the Commerce Department. At the same time the first administrator of the Federal Emergency Relief Administration saw the importance of having a Black attaché.

Many of the agency heads did not approve of the idea, but Blacks were slowly added to one department after another. They had no clear-cut outline of function and were in most cases without authority. Under these circumstances these advisors had the difficult task of changing attitudes of departmental heads and of framing a program within an unfriendly setup in a way to make it acceptable. Once policies were delicately changed to include increased Black participation, wisdom had to be exercised for its implementation. In this way, without authority, they endeavored to convert, to break down barriers and prejudiced transitions in government.

But near the end of Roosevelt's third term in office, white administrators of agencies who revealed too much interest in progressive acts and the integration of Blacks were chased out of office, or their appropriations reduced to an amount that rendered them ineffectual.

Blacks in important government positions were not an innovation. Prior to the administration of Woodrow Wilson, Blacks were appointed to many federal posts, including counselors to Haiti, Nicaragua, Madagascar, Dakar, St. Etienne, Brazil, Sierre Leone, Cognac, and Puerto Cabelle. Formerly, they also held such positions as collector of customs at Charleston, South Carolina; Savannah, Georgia; District of Columbia; and Beaufort, South Carolina; and collector of internal revenue in Hawaii; Atlanta, Georgia; New York City; and Jacksonville,

Florida. At one time a Black served as 4th auditor of the Navy. Blacks also served as receivers of public money in New Orleans, Louisiana; Montgomery, Alabama; and Jackson, Mississippi. Then the offices of public lands in New Orleans and comptroller of port in Louisiana were held by Blacks. These appointive positions called for confirmation by the United States Senate. One by one these positions have gone to whites.

Some astute Washington observers firmly believed, however, that during the New Deal Administration Blacks gained more recognition in the federal government than in private industry. In industry, the competition of Blacks for jobs met bitter resistance from the white worker. And trouble experienced by Blacks in industry had a carry-over in housing and public utilities.

As a result of the economic disadvantages, the Black family had less security than whites and by 1941 a frustration enmeshed Black children, whose resentment was demonstrated in petty violence, mugging, and a general wave of child delinquency. They were denied opportunities for training in skilled jobs. They knew, too, of the difficulty their parents had in getting upgraded in skilled jobs. They were aware of the segregated blood bank policy of the American Red Cross. There were rumors and race scares emanating from every section of the country.

Apprehension of trouble caused Governor Colgate Darden of Virginia to call an off-record meeting in Norfolk with about thirty representative Blacks in September, 1942, for a frank discussion of Black-white relations. Unfounded rumors had circulated among whites that Black domestics had organized into Eleanor clubs for the purpose of murdering white employers for speaking disparagingly about the Roosevelts. This was proved to be false, but the Blacks took advantage of the meeting with the governor and reported their dissatisfaction with the irregular enforcement of laws by civil servants and police officers who acted not as protectors, but as abusers. They expressed discontent over the fact that the state operated institutions for Blacks such as hospitals and sanitariums and that they were manned entirely by white staffs.

In Baltimore, Maryland, difficulties stemmed from an alleged infested political control. It was often heard that the public office holders had boasted of keeping the town "for whites only."

To appreciate the almost unbelievable, one must go back to August 1938, when Thomas R. Smith, a Black, was laid to rest. A news item, "Women Weep at Smith's Bier," by Lula Jones-Garrett, (Baltimore) *Afro-American*, August 20, 1938, gave this report:

> To begin with, he was ruthless in building up his political power and fortune, caring very little about means of accomplishing aims.
>
> He made one of his first political coups by luring Republican voters (Negroes) into his saloon on voting day, locking them in until voting was over.
>
> He is said to have maintained his domination by an elaborate spy setup, which prevented any illegal business being conducted without his knowledge and consent.
>
> Reporting his death on Saturday, one white reporter said that he (Tom Smith) assisted the police in locating criminals, then lent all his aid to assist the accused in getting out of trouble.

Some old Baltimoreans claimed that the political machine Raisen-Gorman-Mahon-Kelly gave Tom Smith his political start. He was the Black controller of all political patronage. Another *Afro-American* report said:

> It was recalled, however, that on one occasion three white men and the late Mr. Smith were accused of taking a ballot box from a polling place and tampering with the ballots.
>
> What became of this charge is now hazy in the memory of those close to the leader at that time. All of his acquaintances admit that during his colorful career as a political lieutenant he had several brushes with the law.
>
> In May 1936, he was arrested on a charge of operating the "Lucky number syndicate" along with two whites. It was alleged that over $370,000 was taken in by this gambling combine every six months.

But State and city officials attended his funeral services.

Even United States Senator George L. Radcliffe spoke in these terms:

I am here today with you, a few of the countless friends of Tom Smith. He and I have had contacts for many years. He has always kept the faith. I am here to pay respects. I will always cherish his memory.

The funeral oration was delivered by the Rev. Frederick Douglas, who said:

I am glad that there are untold thousands, not only of colored but also for white people, who have been the recipients of the benefactions of this man . . . the man whom men and women sought—men and women from clergymen to the sinner and the outcast, in the most obscure alley of Baltimore.

In short, Tom Smith had built up a vice dynasty in consideration for a wholesale control of Black votes. Blacks in positions of leadership could only do shadowboxing in the attack upon him because of their personal obligation or fear of ruin through political intrigue.

During the early days of World War II Baltimore was a tender spot. Police brutality had reached such a point that Blacks began retaliating by the use of arms. The situation reached the point that along Pennsylvania Avenue, one of the main thoroughfares for Blacks, all automobiles were ordered from the street on Saturday evenings as a safety measure for the police, who feared an attack. Conflict, confusion, and rumors were floating in all sections.

Chicago was severely hit by the turmoil of the war years. Chicago was one of the earliest northern cities where Blacks made some sign of progress and whites remained sensitive to their migration. It was the first city to have Blacks appointed and elected to a number of public offices. Blacks developed for a time a flourishing business in the entertainment field. Blacks occupied decent apartment buildings. But during the war period, in many respects Chicago took on the atmosphere of a southern town.

In Detroit, seasoned hard-boiled, labor union organizers

looked upon the brewing unrest of Blacks as alarming and as threatening serious disaster. Already neighborhood fights between Blacks and whites had occurred in playgrounds about Detroit and later city-wide riots occurred.

In Cleveland, one social agency placed a special investigator in the Black community to check the wave of crime in order to avoid the stigma like that of the so-called Harlem crime wave that occupied so much space in the daily press of New York City in 1941. These outbreaks, rumors, and seething trouble were symptomatic of the period.

During this time a new phenomenon in Black journalism came upon the scene. It was Adam Clayton Powell, Jr., minister of Abyssinian Baptist Church, who became editor of *People's Voice*, councilman, leader of the People's Committee. He played politics with all factions and because of his astute maneuvering came out of many difficult situations unscathed. Later he was elected to the House of Representatives—the first Black ever to go from New York State to Congress.

Adam Powell was brought up in one of the largest Black churches in the country. His father had been the minister, and the congregation followed young Powell's activities through college, his growth from youth to manhood, and into taking over the pastorate following in his father's footsteps. As a youth, he was known as a "hell raiser." The congregation understood him and he was forgiven. As minister, his parishioners did not expect him to be a conventional Baptist preacher.

Powell made no bones about being a minister, for he rather liked to start out one of his spell-binding speeches with: "I am a Baptist preacher; give me five minutes and I'll say a helluva lot." He did. Coupled with his gift of speech, he had an unusual insight into mob psychology. He worked it overtime.

Shortly after he took office as the first Black councilman ever elected in New York City, Powell, through the *People's Voice*, called for the abolition of racial barriers against Blacks on faculties in the City College of New York. His data were not all documented and the campaign turned out to be an attack on the college's presidents.

On the heels of the City College campaign, Powell announced through the *People's Voice* that there would be a city-owned public market erected in Harlem. The New York *Age* investigated, and charged that the campaign was a "Powell bubble."

But Adam Powell could get behind an issue and "go to town." For example, a white cop killed an alleged demented Black in attempting to apprehend the Black, a city hospital patient. Powell went into action—the *People's Voice* headlined, "Police Brutality"; a mass meeting was called at The Golden Gates Ballroom, where a Citizens Committee was formed to take legal action . . .

In the course of his Sunday morning service, he announced that Mayor La Guardia had telephoned him to call off the mass meeting because of fear that rioting would break out and it was political suicide. The meeting went off as scheduled. Nothing happened. Three days later Editor Powell's editorial appeared in P.V.—"MICKEY MOUSE VS MAYOR LA GUARDIA—THE WINNER, MICKEY!" The editorial in part read:

> The Mayor of the City of New York is one of the most pathetic figures on the current American scene. Never has a public figure disintegrated so thoroughly as has Fiorello La Guardia . . . . We are ignored.
>
> When every elected political leader of all parties desired an appointment concerning the brutal slaying of Wallace Armstrong, he not only refused to see them, but did not have the decency to acknowledge the telegram.
>
> Now surrounded by the leeches who sold their birthrights for a mess of political appointments, the Mayor still thinks he is great, but the common people—we know different. Some people think he is weakening in mind. IF THE MAYOR RAN AGAINST MICKEY MOUSE TOMORROW FOR MAYOR OF THE CITY OF NEW YORK, HE WOULD BE DEFEATED.

The older, established newspapers were fighting discrimination in government armed services and in public affairs, which pushed Blacks out and denied them the right to work. Many of the newspapers adopted a more vigorous policy of protest.

When France and England declared war on Germany in 1940, Blacks in the United States were again put into a position of combatting overt manifestations of hatred and intolerance. America became the last citadel of democracy, but the

Black became a stepchild in the whole national defense program. Industries called for workers but refused to employ Blacks. An investigation of racial policies of firms holding defense contracts in the area of Kansas City, Missouri, in the middle of 1941, revealed a hostile attitude on the part of the employers in the face of appeals of patriotism and full participation in national defense. This survey conducted by the Kansas City Urban League found that out of fifty-four employers, twenty-seven employed no Blacks and staunchly asserted that they had no intention of changing their policy to include them, notwithstanding the fact that there was a need for additional labor. One firm that acted as a spokesman for the group stated:

We have never employed Negroes in twenty-five years and see no need of doing so now.[1]

In the same manner as management, unions holding closed-shop agreements persistently barred Blacks from membership. This was true despite the international charter of AFL unions, which nobly stated that no exceptions were made because of race, creed, or color.
It was brought out:

For instance . . . the action of the AFL Shipbuilders' Union of Tampa, Florida. This union last Fall succeeded in signing a closed-shop contract with the Tampa shipyard building defense shipping. The union refused membership to 500 shipyard Negroes then employed and enforced its closed-shop agreement by throwing the Negroes out of work. We certainly cannot afford to forget that the International Machinists Association holds contracts with twelve aircraft manufacturing companies and the machinists' union bars Negroes from membership by ritualistic oath.

The Brotherhood of Railway and Steamship Clerks has a

---

[1]*The Negro and Economic Opportunity.* Address delivered by Lester B. Granger before the National Conference of Social Work, June 6, 1941, Atlantic City, N. J.

color clause in its constitution prohibiting the membership of Negro workers. In this connection, the Brotherhood of Railway and Steamship Clerks refuses to give up jurisdiction over the Redcaps and has, in order to maintain the right to collect dues from these employees, get up what is known as auxiliary locals in which the Negro Redcaps only have the right to pay dues, but have no voice in the conventions of the Brotherhood of Railway and Steamship Clerks or to affect the policy of this organization in any way whatsoever. . . . It recognizes the right of taxation without representation. . . .[2]

Of course, this procedure was not followed by all of the unions. Particularly, CIO unions did not deny Blacks the right to membership and only 19 craft unions out of the 103 affiliated with the AFL refused Blacks cards.

Because of this unfavorable industrial situation, A. Philip Randolph addressed an open letter, which appeared in the Black press, to President Franklin D. Roosevelt, calling his attention to the fact that the industries of the country were not making use of and would not consider employing Black labor. In the letter, it was suggested that failure on the part of the president to act in behalf of this large minority would inspire Blacks to dramatize this unfair treatment by marching on Washington en masse. The slogan "March on Washington" caught the imagination of the Black masses, and by popular demand the creator of the idea was called upon to mobilize Blacks from all over the country.

Randolph's leadership was never doubted by Blacks, because of his leadership in organizing the Pullman porters in defiance of one of the richest and most powerful companies in the country.

The march on Washington was scheduled for July 1, 1941, by a sponsoring committee organized by Randolph and including Walter White, executive secretary of the National Association for the Advancement of Colored People; William Lloyd Imes, later president of Knoxville College, but then minister of the (New York) St. James Presbyterian Church; Lester B.

---

[2]*Ibid.*

Granger, executive secretary of the National Urban League; Frank R. Crosswaith, chairman of the Negro Labor Committee; Layle Lane, vice-president of the American Federation of Teachers; Richard Parrish, president of the Metropolitan Association of Negro Students; Rayford Logan, chairman of the State and National Committee for Participation of Negroes in National Defense; J. Finley Wilson, Grand Exalted Ruler of the I.B.P.O.F. of W.; Adam C. Powell, Jr.; Noah A. Walters of the Laundry Workers Joint Board of Greater New York, CIO; E. E. Williams, secretary-treasurer of the Blasters and Drillers Union, AFL; Henry K. Craft, executive secretary of the Harlem Branch YMCA; T. S. Jackson, president of the Dining Car Employees Union and Channing H. Tobias, senior secretary of the National Council of YMCA's.

In a release to the Negro press, Randolph gave the purpose for the march. And the Washington *Tribune*, June 7, 1941, printed the story in part as follows:

> In a democracy every citizen has a right to express his opinion about the policies of the government. He has a right, lawfully and orderly, to seek to change these policies when he deems them inadequate and unjust. This is the purpose of the plan for 100,000 Negroes to march on Washington.
>
> Negroes are rightfully dissatisfied with the Administration's policy or lack of policy on the Negro and defense. We are out to change it.

Must Mobilize

Mass power is the chief form of power Negroes possess if they mobilize it. It is a matter of common knowledge, however, that Negro mass power has never been really tested, measured and utilized to even its approximate maximum pressure possibilities.

When 100,000 Negroes march on Washington, it will wake up Negro as well as white America.

It will stun the government, shock business and astonish organized labor.

I call upon the Negroes everywhere to gird for an epoch-making march and demonstration, July 1, for jobs, justice and freedom in the Nation's capital.

On to Washington!
Let the Negro masses march!
Let the Negro masses speak!

Front-page headlines and space were given freely to the proposed march and editorial.

The (Tulsa) *Oklahoma Eagle*, looked upon the time as ripe for action and did not approve calling off the march without more favorable executive action. The *Eagle*, July 5, 1941, announced that

> Now is the time for action. This is no time for dreams. If it takes an executive order to open the doors of defense industries to the manpower and talent of all the people, let us have the executive order. This is no time for sweet promises or fence straddling. The question of the Negro and defense is not a "race problem." It is a problem of democracy which the government must face now. It will be too late when dictators close their hands on the few remaining free nations.

The (Kansas City, Kans.) *Plaindealer*, June 27, 1941, observed that the veterans of World War I had to march on Washington to force favorable bonus action for them, and other groups that had marched were successful in getting their demand. The *Plaindealer* pointed out that

> So as far as we are concerned we say go ahead with the march. A stand must be taken one way or another, and the Negroes much be prepared to either lose or win. The fight which Negroes are conducting to gain their economic, social and political freedom is a dangerous one and there is no such thing as being in the safety zone. Of course we realize that common sense and good judgment should precede all action. And in this particular instance we feel that to postpone the march in the light of the fact that discrimination and the evils in the war department still exist would not be good judgment.

A change in the attitude by Mrs. Roosevelt gave the movement an additional impetus, for the (National) *Defender*, June

27, 1941, carried an Associated Negro Press release stating that

Mrs. Eleanor Roosevelt again demonstrated her willingness to aid the cause of the Negro when she conferred Friday with A. Philip Randolph and Walter White who are planning a "March on Washington," July 1, to protest silently against the unfair treatment accorded Negroes under the present defense set-up.

It is understood that Mrs. Roosevelt discussed the consequences "good and bad" of the march, and also suggested how "the most effectiveness might be gotten out of the demonstration." Randolph is said to have received two telegrams to date from Secretary of the Navy Knox, but the contents have not been disclosed.

And before the last week in June the Negro press headlined as a moral victory President Roosevelt's famous executive order 8802 banning discrimination against racial or religious groups in defense industries.

Positions were immediately taken by most of them. The May 31, 1941 issue of the New Jersey *Guardian* said:

The March On Washington

The proposed march on washington in protest of defense industry discrimination against employing Negroes appears as the most vivid disclosure of how a tenth of the country's native born citizens are being "blacked out" of the blessings of this great democracy. If we grant that there are a lot of officials in Washington with studied ignorances of prejudiced practices against Negro workers then this demonstration should go a long way towards informing them of its existence. To that other type of official who considered a form letter reply to protests against such practices as sufficient, this march should acquaint him with what vital concern this job ban is to Negroes.

Some of the larger newspapers did not endorse the movement. The *Pittsburgh Courier* launched a double-V campaign, victory at home and victory abroad, which included an independent drive to get Blacks jobs in defense industries. Although the March-on-Washington movement did not openly bar whites from active participation, they were neither invited nor welcomed. This policy of isolation by the leaders of the march caused some of the Black newspapers to act cool toward the mobilization plan. The sentiment in some quarters was so strongly opposed to the self-imposed segregated movement that leaders attempted to explain that the primary effort was to encourage the Black to assume the major responsibility rather than seek the benevolent disposition of a few whites. Whether or not the campaign for the executive order establishing fair employment practices in defense industries tended to have a tinge of racism, there was no carry-over of the policy in the effort to make the Fair Employment Practice Committee permanent. In the lobbying for the legislation, whites as well as Blacks became active. The St. Louis *Argus*, June 13, 1941, commented that

We have stood by so long and looked upon the other fellow enjoying the things to which we were entitled (but denied), until we are becoming desperate. And as Mr. Randolph very properly says, "The Negro is forced to abandon the old method of personal appeal or group appeal to the good will, sympathy and pity of our good white friends."

We urge our readers to read Mr. Randolph's appeal.

Opposition to the mass action of Blacks was expressed by some of the newspapers who disagreed with the proposed strategy. Their position was strengthened when Mrs. Franklin D. Roosevelt advised against the march. Many of the newspapers carried this report on June 20, 1941, under a New York City dateline:

NEW YORK CITY, N. Y.—An important event has taken place in connection with the plan to march on Washington, D. C., by fifty thousand Negroes July 1 in the form of a conference of Mayor LaGuardia of New York; Walter White,

143

A. Philip Randolph and Mrs. Roosevelt. Both Mayor LaGuardia and Mrs. Roosevelt, as friends of the Negroes, have advised that such a march might not obtain the desired results and deeply hurt the Negroes' cause.

And the San Antonio *Register* printed a story in its issue of June 27, 1941 that originated in Washington, D. C., stating that the president opposed the march. The report read in part:

WASHINGTON, D. C.—Pounding the desk with his fist, as he spoke, President F. D. Roosevelt expressed strong disapproval of the proposed "March on Washington," at a White House conference, Wednesday afternoon, June 18, with his calling the proposal "bad and unintelligent."

In the meantime the Black newspapers continued to make editorial comment favoring the March movement. The (Youngstown, Ohio) *Buckeye Review*, June 21, 1941 said in part:

Yes, we should let white America know we are enduring in spite of the fact that we are willing and able to share in our country's defense. Youngstown Negroes will be falling far behind if some of them are not found in the hundreds who will be marching to Washington on July 1.

The (Omaha) Guide, June 21, 1941, saw Randolph as the brilliant and dynamic leader of organizations reaching every element of Black life. The March on Washington, the *Guide* said was:

. . . the culmination of a long fight made by leading Negroes and their papers throughout the country to save America from herself by forcing utilization of the vast productive labor of the LOYAL TENTH of the nation's population.

The (Seattle, Washington) Northwestern Enterprise, June 21, 1941, carried a news release from Washington, D. C. stating that

The whole of the Negro population of the country is aroused and the March on Washington takes on tremendous significance and momentum as the date set for the massing in the nation's capitol of thousands of Negroes draws nearer. . . .

Last week, A. Phillip Randolph, director of the March, received telegrams from Secretary of War Henry L. Stimson and Secretary of the Navy Frank Knox, requesting that he come to Washington for a conference.

The (San Antonio) Register, June 27, 1941, printed a special story from Houston, Texas, telling of the endorsement of the March movement by the National Baptist Sunday School Congress after strong backing by the Rev. William H. Jernagen, president, and the Rev. O. C. Maxwell of New York City.

While the agitation was rapidly increasing, President Roosevelt issued a memorandum to the Office of Production Management urging that office to discourage discriminatory practices. The (St. Louis) Argus, June 20, 1941, expressed the belief:

With these intervening incidents we are inclined to doubt the wisdom of the march because we all know that a statement such as was issued by the President to the officials of the Office of Production Management is bound to get results, sure and certain. Therefore, we think that wisdom would suggest that the proposed march on the capitol as a protest against the injustices which are heaped upon the Negroes in this country should be postponed pending negotiations for more considerations and also to give time for us to see just how much effect the President's words will have with the OPM and the industries.

The (Indianapolis) *Recorder*, June 28, 1941, carried a release from New York City by the Associated Negro Press in which was reported Randolph's rejection of the President's memorandum. The report said:

The statement of the President is one which was expected over 10 months ago. It has no teeth in it and is not a proclamation or executive order which would give assurance of discontinuance of discrimination.

Therefore, the mobilization effort for the March on Washington is being redoubled.

And the Memphis *World*, June 27, 1941, carried an Associated Negro Press release from Washington, D. C., reporting that

Elaborate preparations are being made for the "jobless March on Washington" with the local organization setting up its headquarters in a loft at 7th and S Streets, N. W., where meetings are being held regularly.

The (Boston) Chronicle on June 28, 1941 announced with a streamer headline:

BIG HUB DELEGATION IN MARCH ON CAPITOL

Thursday forenoon, June 19, there was a meeting of the Boston "March on Washington" Committee, under the chairmanship of James H. Jones at the Armstrong-Hemenway Foundation, 43 Rutland Square, of which Julian D. Steele is director.

Enthusiasm ran high and from all indications a large Boston delegation will join in the much publicized march on Washington next week.

Editorially the (Cleveland) *Call-Post* justified the proposed mass demonstration and argued:

We believe the Negro should now take whatever steps are necessary to insure him a bigger participation in the economic life of this nation. If a march on Washington will accelerate the achieving of this goal, then we are for it.

The (St. Louis) American, June 26, 1941, stated that colored Americans were protesting the appalling discrimination against them. Even the pleading of Mrs. Franklin D. Roosevelt, who was esteemed as a friend, was not strong enough to halt the march. The *American* said:

This demonstration should be carried through. Only pressure and protest and organization get results nowadays.

There is no valid reason, none whatever, why Negro workers, all loyal to this country, should be ostracized from the mass production of defense commodities to be used in a war to fight Hitler. Hitler has already prophesied that the very racial intolerances in the U. S. would serve his cause. This must be made another egregious lie by first eliminating the remnants of discriminations here in the democracy of the U.S.

An example of the press release that appeared in the Black newspapers all over the country was carried by its Arkansas *State Press*, July 4, 1941:

HOUSTON, Texas—A. Philip Randolph, president of the Brotherhood of Sleeping Car Porters, dropped a bombshell in the Wednesday night meeting of the 32nd annual conference of the NAACP [National Association for the Advancement of Colored People] when he announced the executive order [8802] issued June 25 banning discrimination in national defense industries.

Mr. Randolph announced that as a result of the order the March on Washington scheduled for July 1 has been postponed. He called the order the greatest thing for Negroes since the emancipation proclamation.

The first public announcement had been made over two national radio hookups previous to the NAACP meeting where Randolph was awarded the Spingarn Medal for outstanding achievement.

To administer the executive order, President Roosevelt created under the Office of Production Management a Fair Employment Practice Committee to consist of six members and subsequently supplemented by an additional member. The personnel of the committee were Malcolm MacLean, president of Hampton Institute; David Sarnoff, president of the Radio Corporation of America; William Green and Philip Murray, presidents of the AFL and CIO, respectively; Earl B. Dickinson and Milton P. Webster of Chicago; and Lawrence W. Cramer, former governor of the Virgin Islands, who was appointed executive director.

The (Omaha) *Star*, June 27, expressed its complete faith in the leadership of the March movement and further assured its readers:

Without a doubt, 50,000 Negroes would have marched on July 1, in a demonstration designed to impress upon the minds of white America that Black America will not relinquish the fight until democracy and liberty in our country becomes real and true.

The Atlanta *Daily World*, the only daily newspaper operated by Blacks in the south, regarded the results as the successful operation of a "lobby of the weak without the more refined advantages of the powerful." Editorially, the *World*, July 5, 1941, warned:

The March Committee Should Now Watch

While all may not have originally favored the proposed March-on-Washington protest organized by able, leveled-headed, and responsible Negro leaders in protest of alarming and widespread discriminations in defense industries and related set-ups, we were inclined to find virtue in it.

It was our opinion that such a monstrous protest would awaken America thunderously, but not injuriously, to the need of binding all sections of the population more closely together by eliminating various types of discriminations creepingly and steadily dividing us. Discriminations are the roots of disunity in a democracy. Nothing, we felt, could be a better contribution to our national unity than a dramatization to America of the Negro's willingness to cooperate in the present crisis. A mass protest against such discriminations in a democracy, we believe, would let the enemies know that their doctrines of slavery hidden in cleverly labeled ideologies were even more obnoxious to these minority groups and would be more strenuously opposed.

Never were we in sympathy with any construction of the "March" as a "make-you-do" movement. We saw it as a lobby

148

of the weak without the more refined advantages of the powerful. We saw it as an inheritance founded in events of history. It was beyond our way of thinking that the "March" would lend comfort to our enemies that America was divided. Open protest is better than silent treachery brought on by a suppression of discontent.

The (New Jersey) *Herald News* could envision Blacks getting a fair hearing after presenting a strong case. On July 5, 1941, the paper commented:

What the Projected March On Washington Did

The projected March of thousands of Negroes on Washington, though it was called off for whatever reasons, was a huge success, as far as we can see.

Organized and projected in the first place to dramatize the unfair, and certainly undemocratic, treatment of American Negro citizens in this period of an announced and undeniable national emergency, the March was never designed merely to increase the foot-wear of the marchers; rather was it designed to gain a hearing for the just demands of the Negro people of this country.

The (San Antonio) *Register* was jubilant over the executive order and felt that it was a point gained by the Black. The reaction of the (St. Louis) *Argus* was one of relief from fear the march would have caused harm. The paper said in an editorial, June 27, 1941, that

The calling off of the march on Washington by the Negroes as a protest against discrimination by the director of the Negro March-on-Washington Committee, A. Philip Randolph, was we think a logical and sensible move. And the committee with which he was working is to be congratulated for its fine judgment at a very critical time in the life and well being of the Negroes in this country.

Thank goodness, that because of the way and manner in which the committee conducted its affairs in preparation of the march, there can be no charge of "selling out" which so frequently follows when leaders change their course for what they regard as the best interests of all concerned.

The (Raleigh) *Carolina Tribune*, July 5, 1941, voiced the opinion that the march had been an absurd proposal. The postponement was received by the editor in his July 5, 1941 issue as follows:

It is good news that the planned "March on Washington" by Negroes anxious for better job opportunities in national defense, and better treatment by bigwigs in the army, navy, marine and air corps, was "postponed" indefinitely from the projected date of July 1st.

The "March" was an absurd idea in the first place, and it is well that it died aborning . . .

We believe in fighting for the same things desired by the proponents of the march but they chose the wrong means. There are more ways to kill a cat than drowning it. It's even possible to choke it to death with butter.

The score was not settled in the opinion of the Louisville *Defender* (July 12, 1941), which stated that grounds for the march on Washington still exist. The *Black Dispatch* looked at the executive order as a half-hearted measure. The *Dispatch* said, July 19, 1941:

Unquestionably there are several weak spots and loopholes in the executive order. In Tulsa last week one of the defense training agencies was obviously evading the "qualifications" clause of the order. Negroes were told that training would not be given to any group unless there was obvious opportunity for such group to be employed. In other words, the Negroes are told that you will not be employed in technical and skilled fields, and therefore, defense training in skilled efforts will not be given you.

The *Black Dispatch* does not believe the order will ever be effective until the President has issued an executive order to NYA, to WPA and to CCC, which compels those administering these federal agencies to give the same and identical training to Negroes as to whites.

We might just as well face the issue. All of the state advisory boards of these agencies are packed with labor union officials who mould policies for Negro training. These labor union heads are determined that Negro youth shall not be placed in competition with skilled white labor.

So long as this continues the great mass of Negroes will remain unskilled. In Oklahoma City sometime ago, when effort was successfully made to organize and charter a carpenter's union, it was discovered that there were only 37 Negroes qualified to join a carpenter's union out of the 20,000 Negroes residing in the Sooner Capital. It can be readily seen that what the Negro needs is training. Without training Negroes cannot expect contractors on federal projects to accept them.

Sooner or later those who seek to integrate Negroes into defense work will discover that the *Black Dispatch* is hitting the nail squarely on the head, when we say the type of discrimination we must fight is the difference in training now given Negroes and whites in NYA and other federally controlled and supervised agencies.

The executive order was actually a compromise, for the original campaign was directed to abolish segregation and discrimination in all departments of government, including the armed services. However, the March on Washington movement stimulated the crusaders of inspired Black newspapers for a first-class citizenship. The attack on government for barring Blacks from the Navy services as cooks was especially vigorous. The attack was almost universal by the papers without any one of them having an understanding with another. It was spontaneous and at one point the Federal Bureau of Investigation had considered bringing a charge of treason against some of the newspapers. And so concerned was the government over the influence of the newspapers that an opinion poll was directed in selected urban centers to ascertain whether Blacks were manifesting sympathies for the Japanese before their attack on Pearl Harbor. The survey also inquired as to what Blacks wanted as citizens, and to whites an inquiry was made as to what they were willing to give up to Blacks.

XII. THE BLACK—A TEST OF DEMOCRACY

After the United States entered World War II, the Black in America reflected the growth of real democracy although his advancement was wedged between many paradoxical situations.

A larger segment of whites than ever known before expressed and demonstrated goodwill toward Blacks. Civic and service organizations that generally avoided problems concerning race relations undertook activities and sponsored programs toward improving the position of Blacks. The daily newspapers began devoting more and more space to Black news other than crime or the basis of its value as news. National periodicals gave an increasing number of pages to a high quality of features about the achievements of Blacks and their successful enterprises. The newspapers published by the Blacks themselves showed an awareness of their importance and their responsibility in better handling of news. Many of them adopted a new creed for raising their professional standards.

Simultaneously with unfavorable incidents during the war, the Black soldiers received big dividends in basic education and specialized training directed by the Army and Navy. This training for the Southern Black youth was significant because of the disparity in educational facilities in the South between Blacks and whites. For instance, the State of Mississippi appropriated no more for Black education in 1945 than it did in 1883. A Black newspaperman observed that in the armed services as late as 1941 there were no Black flyers, but that at the close of actual fighting in Europe and Japan, Blacks were in most of the services. And the Army made a study and then recommendations toward eventually ending its discriminatory practices. Until the war was well advanced the Navy did not open its door to Blacks beyond menial categories. The Navy now has commissioned officers and has abolished its segregation and discrimination policies.

Southern Congressional representatives were persistent during the war period in their attempt to abolish the Fair Employment Practice Committee. They were adamant in blocking the elimination of the poll tax for the privilege of voting and unyielding in the retention of the "White Supremacy" rule reinforced by the Democratic primaries, which for all practical purposes disenfranchised the Black. The United States Supreme Court in one decision on April 1944 ruled that it was unconstitutional to bar Blacks from the primaries.

Three months after the Court ruling, Georgia refused ballots to Blacks who had complied with all the requirements for voting. No incidents took place, and that is the significant fact denoting Black advancement. In the leading daily Atlanta, Georgia newspaper, a column read in part:

Whatever may be the final legal interpretation of our present plan for a 'white primary', it is so obviously an annulment of the purpose and spirit of our Constitution that it cannot stand against the growing sentiment of an enlightened democratic conscience.

A northern correspondent representing an outstanding liberal newspaper wrote that

The cheerful part . . . is that the Georgia people don't seem to carry . . . chips around on their shoulder (about the Negro voting in Primaries), like they do the issue of segregation and a lot of other things.

A Black newspaper reported in an item dated from Dallas, Texas, in July 1944, that for the first time since Reconstruction days, a Black voted in the Democratic primary. The southern states were reluctantly yielding to law and the Supreme Court's last decision on the primary was a step forward for the Black.

In comparison with other sections of the country, the South has shown a lag in "social consciousness." And it is an important advance when southerners themselves acknowledge this fact and act to remedy the condition. That happened when fifty-eight Blacks meeting in Durham, N. C., October 1942, issued a manifesto stating, "What the Black wants and is expecting of the post-war South and nation." And five months later a group of 125 southern whites assembled in Atlanta, Ga., and accepted the document because they considered the

153

statement "so frank and courageous, so free of any suggestion of threat and ultimatum . . . that we gladly agree to co-operate." The southern whites further accepted the Black manifesto as just and publicly expressed the opinion that

> . . . it is a wicked nation that the struggle by the Negro for citizenship is a struggle against the best interests of the nation. To urge such a doctrine, as many are doing, is to preach disunity and to deny the most elementary principles of American life and government.

Black newspaper editors of the South took a very active part in the original conference and when the two groups appointed committees to have joint meetings, P. B. Young, Sr., president of the (Norfolk) *Journal and Guide*, and Carter Wesley, president of the *Houston Informer*, were among the Black conferees. Some northern Black editors censured the southerners for not inviting northern representatives. However, the southern editors answered that the South had to work out its own salvation. But this argument was countered with the fact that the South cannot solve its problem alone, for the section is an integral part of the whole country. And the mobility of population prevents a static condition. When Southerners—white or Black—move into other sections, citizens are affected and concerned, for the patterns to which newcomers are often accustomed differ radically from those of the North.

One distinguished Southern educator, Dr. Frank P. Graham, president of North Carolina University, as a member of the wartime National War Labor Board, wrote the body's decision to eliminate the wage differential between Black and white labor, thus placing the Black worker, especially in the South, on a parity with the white worker in the same classification. Dr. Graham stated in part: "It is rather a bit of realization of the no less sound American principle of equal pay for equal work as one of those equal rights in the promise of American democracy regardless of color, race, sex, and religion or national origin."

In general the South has been slow in improving Black-white relations, but in the fall of 1943 the electrocution of a fourteen-year-old Black boy in South Carolina moved the white editor of a Miami, Fla., daily newspaper to take the position that "We have long advocated white supremacy in the South . . . we could scarcely feel otherwise. But we must confess our stomach sickened when we read the other day that South Carolina had executed a 14-year-old Negro child. What an indictment against South Carolina and its people . . . It's the best proof that State rights can justifiably be curtailed. Such a thing could not have happened in enlightened States." The editor went on to say that he believed that Florida could not stand for such "justice." And he said: "Thank goodness most everybody we've talked to feels that same way. Otherwise we would be horribly ashamed of our fellow Americans who are citizens of South Carolina. Anyway, we feel like apologizing for them—and their inaction against officials who are so ignorant and brutal."

Another white southern newspaper editor, Virginius Dabney, the (Richmond, Va.) *Times-Dispatch,* distinguished himself as a crusader for better Black-white relations in the South. And in an editorial, Sunday, November 21, 1943, wrote in part:

The *Times-Dispatch* advocates abolition of the segregation law on streetcars and buses in Virginia because it considers this the truly conservative course. Such abolition would be tangible and convincing evidence that the whites of Virginia desire to work with the Negroes in eliminating injustices, arriving at amicable solutions of interracial problems, and relieving interracial tension.

Southern Negro leaders are genuinely and sincerely anxious to co-operate with Southern white leaders, and they want to avoid the interracial friction which would be sure to arise, if more radical Negroes from the North should gain a foothold among the colored people of this section. Many Virginians probably do not know it, but we have now arrived at the point where radicals from the North will find it easy to secure a large following in the South, unless reasonable and proper concessions to the colored people are made.

According to the Associated Negro Press in a release on April 8, 1945, a letter was published in the (Charleston) *News and Courier* that had been written by a white man of Frogmore, South Carolina in which he claimed that he was "fed up and sick" with the newspaper's editorial bias against Blacks. The letter signed by F. R. Ford read:

Seventy-two years ago I was born free and white and for more than 40 years, since I became a resident here I have read the News and Courier and expect to continue to read it as long as I read any paper, but I can not refrain from saying I am fed up and sick from your damnable harping on the Negro, his shortcomings and the fact that he is here and can't help it.

Your sneering editorial, 'Detroit Gates Not Ajar,' in today's issue is the barb so constantly applied that drive those you describe as 'well disposed and contented colored people' into the class you describe as those who fancy themselves victims.

You, of course, are willing to admit of your superiority over this strange being you find so necessary to waste your ink and paper lambasting daily. If you will admit you are superior, for God's sake manifest it by ceasing your meaningless mouthing.

Another practice followed by white dailies that created bad race feelings was that of identifying Blacks when they were involved in criminal cases. And the feeling exists among Blacks that this casts a reflection upon the whole race. A prominent Philadelphia lawyer, Raymond Pace Alexander, questioned the editorial policy of the (Philadelphia) *Daily News*; and the publisher, Lee Ellmaker, wrote:

In common justice it is only fair that race, nationality, or religion should not be used in the identification of any person in the news—save where there is a specific reason for additional data. For instance, mention of the fact that the late Dr. Carver was a Negro added to his honor—or the fact that the central figure in the famous Connecticut abduction case of a few years ago was a Negro house-boy was essential to the story.

Under ordinary condition, however, it is unnecessary to identify a person injured in an accident, burned in a fire, arrested in a robbery or figuring in other routine news.

It is impossible to lay down any iron-clad rule but a good policy to follow is to use the word Negro only under circumstances which would call for identification terms of "White," Chinaman, Indian, Protestant, Catholic, Jew, etc.

The publisher's response to the lawyer revealed also another practice that had not been overcome in the news reports that appeared in the dailies. Like the publisher, white reporters spelled "Negro" with a small "n", a practice which failed to follow the rule for writing a proper name.

The Los Angeles Sentinel, April 26, 1945, published this criticism of the white press by one of the Sentinel's foreign correspondents:

By George Coleman Moore Somewhere in Germany

Since D-Day in Europe more than one million words (a week) have been written by newspapermen covering the achievement, valor and heroics of American soldiers. This mountain of verbiage is equivalent to 1,700 full length novels per week.

Also since the invasion date an estimated three million feet of movie film has been recorded and approximately 1½ million photos have been taken for home consumption.

Of this great mass of material submitted by hundreds of reporters, photographers, magazine writers, radio script authors and broadcasters only a little less than two per cent has been deleted by hardboiled censors.

These modern day historians play a tremendous role in information, educational services and the shaping of public opinion. Words are weapons that can explode with the thunder of centuries of reaction or the power of truth and progressivism. Therefore the consideration here is what have these chroniclers been writing about the contribution of Negro troops and what amount of space have home publications given their activities.

Civilian newspapers seldom get to us but we have some editions now from the daily press that appear to be typical. One is from the deep south, another from the middle west and one from the east. Items about Negroes are scarce but when found run in this vein:

One story of a FA outfit is included. Enlisted personnel is quoted in atrocious dialect and are saying the most ridiculous things. Again an officer with an engineering unit is quoted. He is placed in a ludicrous situation and likewise is making absurd statements.

A New York newspaper, the *Daily Mirror*, in a double column editorial, October 16, 1944, struck back at President Roosevelt in his campaign for re-election for his fourth time by inciting a racial issue. A poster released through the CIO Political Action Committee showed a Black and a white riveter appealing to citizens to register. And the *Mirror* observed:

> One very large poster shows us what purports to be the face of President-Candidate Roosevelt wearing goggles and having a large helmet of some kind on his head. Alongside of him is a Negro, also helmeted . . . This poster is plainly an appeal to prejudices.

In an editorial that was carried by the (Norfolk) *Journal and Guide*, a Boston daily newspaper was censured for its handling of a news story about a Black that the Black newspaper considered as creating bad race relations. The editorial looked critically upon the metropolitan newspapers that incite race hatred. It read in part:

> In its 1944 annual forum the (New York) *Herald-Tribune* discussed different phases of the Black problem. One of the chief speakers, Lillian Smith, author of "Strange Fruit," interpreted the "problem" as a "desperate feeling of inferiority" in the white race, which causes it to proclaim its own superiority. Justice Francis E. Rivers, the first Black appointed to the City Court bench in New York City, spoke on "The Racial Question and Anti-poll Tax Measures." Governor J. J. Broughton of North Carolina talked about "Poll Taxes and Voting Rights."
>   A certain amount of interracial friction, and even violence, in parts of the country is to be expected during this war, given the slogans of this global conflict and the emphasis placed by Messrs. Roosevelt and Churchill upon the "four

freedoms." There were serious riots in the first World War, and their recurrence is not surprising. But those of us who edit newspapers can do our bit toward smoothing the points of friction, if we will try to grasp the viewpoint of thinking Negro, and seek tő print the news about his face in an understanding and objective manner.

Too many of us newspapermen think of our colored friends largely in terms of their police court performances, their crap-shooting proclivities and their virtuosity with the razor. We stress this side of the race and forget that there is another, and a more important side.

Those of us who follow the New York press (and who doesn't?) are aware that even in Gotham there are great newspapers which failed notably before the recent Harlem disorders to give their readers the proper perspective on New York City crime. In fact, a prominent Southern Negro, whose judgment I respect highly, said some months before the outbreaks in Harlem: "I have never seen anything that was so subversive, so ridiculous and so damaging as the smear campaign—the artifically created and manufactured campaign—that was carried on by the New York papers about crime in Harlem." There were exceptions, but the overall record of the New York press left something to be desired. Southern newspapers have their own shortcomings to answer for, but this distinguished colored leader said he had never seen or heard of anything like it in the Southern press, except in Atlanta in 1906, when a newspaper's incendiary stories and editorials brought on the great Atlanta riot of that year.

The intelligent Negro also likes to see some notice given in the press to the part his race is playing in the war. If the white papers can't chronicle all the operations of Negro units overseas, as staff correspondents of Negro papers are doing, they can publish accounts of the more noteworthy feats of colored fighting men—such as Dorie Miller, the mess boy who grabbed a machine gun at Pearl Harbor, and won the Navy Cross for heroism. The role of Negro men and women in the war effort is described regularly by such Southern papers as the Mobile, Ala., *Register* and the Shelby, N. C.,

159

Star. It gives Negro readers the feeling that their work in defense of democracy is appreciated.

One of the prime headaches of many Southern newspapers, and of Northern ones as well, is to be found in the use of the titles "Mr.," "Mrs.," and "Miss" where colored people are concerned. While "Professor" and "Doctor" are not considered serious problems, "Mr.," "Mrs.," and "Miss" often cause heavy head-scratching on the part of editors. The simplest and best rule would seem to be that these titles ought to be accorded when the person referred to is of such standing in the community as to warrant it, the rule being much the same for white persons. Educated men or women, perhaps with college degrees and achievements in the arts and sciences, cannot be handled as illiterate swineherds. Both Richmond papers regularly accord the foregoing titles to colored persons of standing. Any other course is strongly resented by the colored community, and rightly so.

Another matter which may not seem to have any special significance, but which is deemed important by our colored friends, is the capitalization of the word "Negro." Members of that racial group feel that only through a capital "N" can the race be given its proper typographical status. Many papers, both North and South, capitalize the word, but others do not. It should be done.

Some colored people appear to object to the mere statement in the body of a crime story that the criminal is a Negro. Two or three New York papers announced recently that they will not use the race tag anywhere in their accounts of crime. This seems an extreme point of view, since the question whether a criminal is white or colored is a material part of the story. However, neither Richmond paper uses the word "Negro" in any headline dealing with crime, and the body of the story contains only one reference to the racial identity of a Negro criminal. This procedure, which seems only fair, has to be modified in rare instances where the racial identity of those concerned is an essential part of the story, but it holds good for ordinary purposes.

What the editors of America need to do primarily in this crisis is to be fair, just and objective in their handling of Negro news, and at the same time to be bold, imaginative

160

and forthright when misunderstanding and misrepresentation seem likely to bring a head-on clash. It has been demonstrated that this approach allays friction, quiets apprehension and helps to create cordial relations and a spirit of national unity.

In view of the criticism that the white newspapers omitted general news about Blacks of an elevated sort, Saville Davis of the *Christian Science Monitor* had this to say:

Essentially, what we are looking for is to assimilate Negro news into the normal flow of the news. It is a simple problem. The Negro simply should be included in the stream of ordinary living. Where there are sidewalk interviews, we should include Negro opinions. There should be news pictures of Negro housewives struggling with ration problems. There would be pictures of Negro and white children playing together—not as a novelty, but as though it were the most natural thing in the world. There should be housing problems of Negroes considered on the same basis as housing problems of any others. The whole emphasis should be on normal relationships . . .

We can no longer live as a society with our economic sins, because they bring about things called maladjustments, saturated markets, imperfect flow of purchasing power—undramatic things, but deadly enemies of the system. We cannot live with our social sins any more. They cause social and political pressures which upset the whole delicate mechanism of our modern society and bring it to collapse.

Our principles, moreover, are catching up with us. We have said just once too often that men are equal. There is a ferment—a moral chemicalization, an economic chemicalization—in the land, and the solution has begun to work. The very constructive tone of the editorials which I read in a select number of Negro newspapers are indications that this is the case, and that there is an alternative to the resort ultimately to blood and the sword in solving this problem.*

Another southern newspaperman, M. D. Potter, publisher of

*Speech before the Negro Press Conference at Hotel Pennsylvania, New York City, May 7, 1943.

the Tampa *Bulletin,* had given thought to the problem of Black-white relations as they are influenced by newspapers. He pondered that most of the trouble arises because the white press considers that its primary function is to serve white people and the Black press feels that its strict duty is to fight for Black people. Thus, as you see, good news, except in rare cases, of one race is hardly ever published in the other press.

Horace Cayton, author and columnist of the *Pittsburgh Courier,* wrote in a letter to the editor of the Chicago *Sun,* September 29, 1943, that the daily newspaper was exceptional in reporting news concerning the mistreatment of Black soldiers. He stated that

The usual explanation for refusing to report the mistreatment of Negro soldiers and sailors; the humiliations which are heaped upon Negro women in the WACS; and the numerous Negroes who have been sentenced to long-term imprisonment for even speaking out against these conditions, is that it would lower the morale of the Negro population.

It is my opinion that this is a fallacious argument. In the first place, white people who are in general unaware of these facts cannot interpret the behavior of Negro civilians and soldiers in certain tension areas. In the second place, Negro soldiers and Negro civilians, seeing that the news which is so disturbing to them is not even published in white papers are not interested in their problems.

The failure of the press to discharge its moral obligation to present the truth, both by not giving full coverage and by editing the news either editorially or by selection, is to destroy the most effective method we have in this society of continuing our struggle for a full democracy. In many instances, the Army's treatment of the Negro is undemocratic to an extreme. Unless brought to light by the newspapers, these practices will spread to the white soldiers and throughout the entire army.

Further, it is pointless to continue to mistreat Negro soldiers and embitter a tenth of our entire population. Negroes of themselves are a relatively minor problem. The large issue is that we are allowing Germany and Japan to turn hundreds of millions of people who do not happen to be Anglo-Saxon against us by our treatment of the American Negro and especially the American Negro soldier.

In my opinion, such a frank, forthright news coverage as the *Sun* carried in the September 27, 1943 issue, and such an editorial as was carried on the shooting of a Negro soldier in Selvridge Field are steps toward a more healthy attitude in the treatment of Negro news.

But Cayton's praise of the Chicago *Sun* put the newspaper in a different category from the majority of the dailies in the country. A white columnist of the Chicago *Defender* (June 2, 1945), Earl Conrad, made an attempt to find out the relations of the white press to the actual handling of Black news. In his column, "Yesterday and Today," he took particular notice that:

Some 200 Negro weeklies stand in relation to the daily press and the big news services in much the same way that Negro passengers on a Southern bus sit in relation to the whites. The Negro press tags along behind the dailies completely Jim Crowed, with the white press often not knowing that Negro journalism even exists. Sometimes I have wondered about the Jim Crow arrangement that places the Negro in back where he can watch the whites. Such trust! Wouldn't you think that the whites, if they must Jim Crow, would place the Negro up front where he can be observed?

In the case of the press this seemingly curious little observation bears a great truth. On the Negro press there is a live awareness of the white press and what it is doing and saying, especially as it concerns the Negro. Indeed, the Negro press devotes much space to interpretive reaction to the activities portrayed in daily, white journalism.

In order to filter favorable news about Blacks into dailies, especially the metropolitan press, Conrad secured interviews with distinguished whites on subjects dealing with race relations. His selection of personalities was also based on those accepted as good news copy by daily newspapers. Conrad had these interesting results:

Press Agent For Negro Press

I have considered that one of the possible functions I might be able to help with, in joining the Negro press, would be to "press agent" the Negro press to its white brothers, to help break down the rigid caste line that separates these two opposed and hostile forces—for they do oppose each other. Although the Negro press receives the "silent treatment," the hostility between the two journalisms, "the caste struggle" (as Gunnar Myrdal calls it) is vitally apparent from reading any Negro weekly front page.

With that thought in mind—to breach the barrier between the two journalisms—I deliberately interviewed Prof. Albert Einstein and secured from him a statement on the supremacy issue which I naively supposed the white press would rush to grab up! I thought a statement from this great citizen of America and of the world would be powerful enough to break through the conspiracy of silence. Knowing that the clash of individuals with institutions sometimes makes news, I felt that I could relay Einstein's statement to the great news services and the wide-reaching dailies, and cross the gulf. Here is what happened:

I wired 14 major newspapers, press services and networks, and urged them and invited them to pick up the historic Einstein statement. My telegram conveyed enough information to indicate it was a major pronouncement from a man whose words, on whatever subject, have always interested the world. And there were a few interesting reactions: The *Daily Worker* and *PM* each carried good news stories repeating Einstein's main thesis on white supremacy. But generally there was a silence, no word from the New York dailies, and a lone inquiry to see the Einstein message from *Newsweek*. It was evident to me that the New York press had decided Einstein stepped out of bounds.

Wire Service Uses Story

I sent a second wire, this time to 20 organizations and individuals charging "deliberate suppression of the most important statement on social relations made by Einstein since he has been in America," and inviting anyone interested to inquire about the details of the suppression. This promptly drew a reply from the Associated Press pointing out that it had sent out a story, and enclosing it. It was a three-paragraph item, so brief or so inadequate that no New York paper picked it up. But it was used around through the country—and the gap had been bridged! Although most of the New York City dailies are a very guilty lot, I found out this:

1. The white press can and will use Negro news.

2. It is possible to smash the silent treatment.

3. It is possible to teach the metropolitan press and the news agencies that the biggest story in America is "the caste struggle."

4. The gap between the white press and the Negro press can be bridged. Often there is not willful neglect on the white side, but unawareness (if I may use a polite word for ignorance). There is good will and good intention in many quarters and it must be unearthed.

5. When the big news services and big dailies begin telling this biggest story of all—which they'll have to, if the FEPC movement takes root properly—America will advance with great new haste.

The Writer's War Board and its Committee to Combat Race Hatred commissioned Columbia University's Bureau of Applied Social Research to make a study in 1944 of the treatment accorded white, Protestant Anglo-Saxons in mass media as against that accorded other minorities. The research report concluded about daily newspapers in their treatment of the Black that

The press—in the North is, with some notorious exceptions, generally fair, although not zealous where minorities are concerned. About 60% of the Southern press is considered anti-Negro despite all disclaimers.

The Black newspapers concentrated on their campaign against discrimination, but some of the newspapers failed to grasp the significant social change of the period and often combined important events with stories intended to build up circulation.

165

Some of the newspapers in deploring unfavorable conditions failed to employ at times the best strategy for gaining desired ends. Often some of these newspapers, imitating the sensational headline trend of the general press, went overboard. These newspapers were severely criticized during the war for the bad handling of some stories but none of the critics who were interested in achieving better conditions wanted the papers to lessen their militancy.

Thomas Sancton, as managing editor of *The New Republic*, in a special article appearing in the April 26, 1943 issue, analyzed the Black press and in his opinion:

When a white man reads a Negro newspaper, it is like getting a bucket of cold water in the face. There is hardly a white man alive—whether a product of the Emerson tradition and the abolitionist soil of Harvard, or whether of Mississippi Delta—who is not a ruddy sahib in his heart. If we get to understand this fact about ourselves, we can disarm it. It would do many a Southerner and many a South-hating Yankee sahib a lot of good to take a look at the Negro paper. The Negro writers, over and over, in all possible variations, with a variety of tones and shadings, with none of the ambiguous and deceitful language by which hard facts are softened in the white press, tell the Negro exactly what the white man is doing for him and to him. It is not a bad thing for a white man to see how he looks through Negro eyes, and it is even better for him to try to understand why it is so . . .

The fundamental weakness of the Negro press is its strong tendency to overcompensate. Where Negro achievement is slighted in the white press, it is overpraised in the race press. Negro crime is apt to be given subjective and apologetic treatment. Most white newspapers in New York have overplayed and emphasized recent robberies and assaults in Harlem, suggesting that race, rather than deplorable social conditions, was responsible. The Negro press in New York has been carried to another extreme in its reaction against these stories. They have counterattacked the white man on the basis of his own criminal record, and have tried to explain away Harlem's numerous recent crimes and their causes. Where the Negro race is systematically disparaged in the

166

white press (frequently unintentionally or through ignorance) and the white man given the benefit of every doubt,
the reverse is true in the Negro press. There are two ways
of looking at such overcompensation; one is to say superfi-
cially that its fundamental cause is the white man's treatment of the Negro; but it is far more important to the Negro
people and to the goals they hope to achieve that the men
who write for the Negro press rise to a larger point of view
than the eye-for-an-eye philosophy . . .
Racism is a bad game no matter who plays it. Despite such
outspoken features as the better-conduct campaign, or the
fact that much of the criticism of white affairs is justified,
there is an accompanying tendency to create a chauvinistic
racism among the Negro people, and a feeling of subjective
bitterness towards all whites.

Even in the early part of 1945, A. Philip Randolph cautioned
Black newspapers to guard against racism. The statement appearing in the February 2 issue of the (Cleveland) *Herald* said
that

My attention has been called to an article on Jews which
recently appeared in a Negro weekly. The title of the article
was "The Indigestible Jew," and it contained a number of
statements which both amazed and pained me. Of all people,
Negroes should be the last to cast any aspersions on another
minority group, which more often than not is the target of
the poisoned arrows aimed at us as well. It is this consideration which prompts me to write the following lines.
It behooves us to be doubly careful not to do anything that
would tend to arouse prejudice against other groups. The
Negro press should be especially on the alert against mis-
leading items concerning our neighbors. We resent such
items in the general press when they reflect unfairly and
unjustly against the Negro community. Well, the same rule
obtains with respect to other groups, including members of
the Jewish faith.

Many Black leaders who followed the course of the Black

press resented sharply criticism of the newspapers because, as one remarked, it

> plays right into the hands of enemies of the Negro and of democracy by completely ignoring the facts that the Negro press unearths, checks and publishes facts about mistreatment of Negroes which otherwise would never see the light of day.

Editorially, the New York *Age*, June 20, 1942, commenting on the treatment of Blacks in the news columns of daily newspapers in New York, touched a point that is common in many communities:

> Many Negroes feel that the daily press has become so liberal in its treatment of Negro news that there is little need for a Negro newspaper, especially in New York. Paced by *PM,* the Marshall Field tabloid, the daily press has been publishing an increasing amount of news about Negroes, and not all of this news has been about crimes committed by Negroes.
>
> But if anyone feels that the daily press of New York will publish any news story about Negroes, they should consider the treatment of the mass meeting held by the March on Washington Committee in protest against the continued discrimination against and Jimcrowism of Negroes in both defense industries and in the armed forces of the nation.

The Black press in some situations showed an inclination to guard against handling stories that would be labeled as inflammatory. Disturbances in industrial cities, marking open resentment by whites of Black competition and the agitation by subversive groups operating against the war effort, broke out in various sections of the country. A riot in Detroit, the industrial capital of America, was an occasion for the Black press to have made use of large headlines and vituperative editorials. But the newspapers handled the situation with astuteness.

These conflicts were viewed by the editor of the (Cleveland) *Call-Post* as the fulfillment of Hitler's dream for unrest and revolt in the United States. While the editor of the *Los Angeles Sentinel* considered the riots

> As if to balance good news of military successes almost everywhere in our global war, a rash of race riots—so severe that no amount of story book optimism can conceal their racial character—has broken out to shame our nation and to furnish grist for Goebbels's propaganda mills.

And the (Iowa) *Bystander* looked at the Detroit riot as a disgrace to the nation and felt that it was proof that

> We don't practice in America what we are fighting the Axis power for doing; that we are unwilling to assume prompt leadership, thus enabling situations to get out of control . . .

These disorders prompted the (Boston) *Guardian* to recall that Hitler called Americans cowards because we were bombing Germany when out of reach of Nazi bombers. Since Hitler could not wreck our industries by bombs, the *Guardian* accused him of disrupting war production by plotting and promoting riots.

The editor of the *Black Dispatch* analyzed the situation as a war hysteria that challenged every American citizen to uproot the evil:

> At first blush one might assume that the fundamental disorders now shaking the very foundations of American society are wholly basic in race prejudice, but this is entirely beside fact and truth. Take, for example, coal strike orders of John L. Lewis having nothing to do with anything other than wage scales for union mine workers, or the struggle in congress today regarding poll tax laws that disfranchise more than nine million white citizens down in Dixie. These cannot be characterized as racial disturbances, although these two struggles alone have American society almost frantic with their repercussions.
>
> Congress adjourned the other day in a boisterous uproar when Mississippi's John Rankin objected to appropriating

funds for the relief of a Jew. In the stress of war our national legislators indulged in a few hours of Jew-baiting.

Everywhere one turns he finds frayed nerves and an absence of poise and social balance. As we said at the outset, "Democracy is in labor." When intolerance shoves up its ugly head we should immediately start thinking objectively. Today, minority groups should start thinking of meeting intolerance with tolerance and impatience with patience. One who thinks for the future can do this. If out of this terrible hour democracy is actually born, there will be copious dividends repaying those who have clarity of vision and understanding in these hours of social confusion.

The dean of Black newspaper editions, P. B. Young, Sr., who had taken an active leadership in race relations in the South, counseled with a mixed group of Black and white editors on the question of the Black newspapers' handling of news. He reflected:*

If you have followed the Negro Press, you have noticed that there has been a unanimity of attitude on the part of all Negro newspapers in this country. It is a thing that has just happened, and it happened because, at this time, as at no other time in the history of America, the Negroes of this country are united on all questions that affect them as Americans and as citizens of this nation.

There is no difference of opinion among the Negroes. There may be shades of opinion; there may be differences of technique and of procedure. Some may be a little more conservative than others. Some have had more experience than others, have been knocked around a little more than others. Some are gray from worry and work. But there is no difference of opinion among the Negroes in America as to what the Negro is entitled to under the Constitution and the laws of this country, as a citizen of this country. And there is no difference among them as to their determination ultimately to achieve what they are entitled to as American citizens.

*Speech before the Negro Press Conference at Hotel Pennsylvania, New York City, May 7, 1943.

Saville R. Davis examined a selected number of editorials appearing in Negro newspapers expecting

"To find on their editorial pages words which would call a great many of us on the white press things which we should deserve to be called—bloody, blistering, blasted so-and so's."

He observed that . . . I would not have quarreled if you had said those things. But what do I find? I find language which is about as reasonable and about as constructive as anybody could possibly ask for on an editorial page.

These articles, then—which, I say, are only typical samples of what I have found in these editorial pages of all these papers—would seem to indicate that the leadership in the Negro press is first recognizing the responsibility for promoting revolution—if I can use the word "Revolution" in the sense that there is a revolution in our social life which is now fermenting and coming to the fore.

Secondly, they appear to recognize very keenly their responsibility for controlling that revolution and making sure that it does not divide and lead directly to war, without the alternative of reasonable compromise between men of strong opinions.

I used the word "compromise." That probably was a very badly chosen word, I don't say that there should be appeasement, in any fashion whatsoever. My newspaper and I, as an individual, stand against appeasement internationally and stand against appeasement on any moral issue of great importance, such as the Negro issue.

I can only say, then, that I find it somewhat difficult as a representative of a moderate newspaper which seeks always to stress the conservative to make any comments whatsoever on the Negro editorial page on the basis of evidence of samples.

The point is that all of these editorials have been based upon ideas and the presentation of ideas. They have not been based upon name-calling and the purely hating type of writing which drives in the direction of civil war. I sense, therefore, a degree of maturity in these papers which, I regret to say, does not always exist in the newspapers with which I am immediately acquainted.

There are editors who recognized that the strategy of their papers had to be altered with rapidly changing conditions. One of the editors, Carter Wesley, observed at the Negro Press Conference that

So highly have we developed the technique of protest and bombast, and so wholly have we accepted that as a technique of Negro leaders that it has become a crime to attempt to be sane, sensible, and effective by taking what you have and working in a manner to get what you want. I don't think we should retreat a single step in our demands for equality and democracy, but I don't believe that we have to get mad everytime we discuss it. A friend of mind in Oklahoma used to say, "A mad man can't make money." Neither do I believe a mad man can ever influence people to do what he wants as well as a sane, calm, courageous, positive man can.

But E. Washington Rhodes, son-in-law of the late Chris Perry and now publisher of the Philadelphia *Tribune*, countered criticism against the papers in these words:

The only thing that we Negroes want in America, and the only reason for the existence of the Negro press, is to get some equality in America and break down discrimination. Perhaps we are not doing the best job. Perhaps some other people might do a better job than we are doing. They might be able to make a *New York Times* out of some of our papers, but I don't see how that is possible right at this minute.

We are crusading papers. So far as I am concerned, I am a crusader, because I dislike to be discriminated against. I dislike to be set apart as something different when all of my reactions are just like any other American's.

In facing some issues, Blacks have been fearless, courageous, and intelligent. P. B. Young, Sr., of the Norfolk *Journal and Guide*, crusaded for better educational facilities, health facilities, and civil rights of Blacks in the South. And G. James Fleming in the July 1938 *Crisis,* said:

There are editors like Roscoe Dunjee of the *Black Dispatch* in Oklahoma, who have had to issue their papers—with a shotgun nearby but who have continued bravely, their heart and soul in their high calling and not worried whether there shall be meat and potatoes for Sunday's dinner.

In an analysis of front pages of twenty-eight Black newspapers that appeared in *Fortune* magazine, May 1945, James S. Twobery pointed out that there were virtually no stories that dealt with white people exclusively. The *Fortune* analysis showed that the Black-white and Black stories appeared in the following proportions:

Stories	Southern papers	Papers outside the South	Total
Reporting or furthering friendly Negro-whites relations..........	40%	32%	35%
Unfavorable to whites' conduct of Negro-white relations	13	21	18
Neutral in attitude on Negro-white relations......................	<u>13</u>	<u>16</u>	<u>15</u>
Total on Negro-white relations	66%	69%	68%
News exclusively about Negroes	<u>34</u>	<u>31</u>	<u>32</u>
Total of all front-page stories.................	100%	100%	100%

A listing of articles exclusively about Blacks in *Fortune's* analysis and comments follows:

Stories	Southern papers	Papers outside the South
Social, church, clubs.............	7.8%*	6.2%
Education..............................	6.7	2.2
Negro betterment..................	3.8	1.4
Charity.................................	2.2	1.2
Business...............................	2.5	.9
Labor....................................	1.5	.5
Total Group 1.................	24.5	12.4%
Crime....................................	2.8	7.3
Deaths, births, illness..........	1.8	3.4
Disaster................................	.2	.6
Total Group 2.................	6.5	13.1
Foreign news........................	.6	1.2
National News......................	.9	.7
Miscellaneous.......................	1.0	3.3
Total Group 3................	2.5	5.2
Total all groups......	33.5%	30.7%
	(i.e. 34%)	(i.e. 31%)

*These are very high percentages particularly since they represent front-page news only. The exclusion of Black social events from the white press makes Black society reporting one of the main functions of the Black press.

The point of this table is that stories of the sort here classified in Group 1 usually predominate in white papers appealing to the upper-income and educational levels, while stories of the sort found in Group 2 characterize the press that appeals to the lower-income and educational levels among the white population. That the situation should be reversed in the Black press suggests that perhaps the southern Black, however great his absolute disadvantages may be for the moment, is, either from choice or from force of circumstances, more conservative. The phenomenon may be a hangover from the plantation feudalism—the "yassah, massa" attitude. In its extreme form it is the current despair of fighters for Black equality, who brand it "good niggerism." The label cannot, however, fairly be applied to the southern Black press, since it gives almost as much attention to Black-white relations as does the rest of the Black press. But, because of its environment, it must be far more cautious about what it prints.

The *Fortune* press analysis pointed out that

Stories	Southern papers	Papers outside South
Training, promotions, social notes, defense of Negro rights, etc.,	11%	6%
Battle activities, deaths in service, other war news	14	9
Total reflecting favorably on the armed services..................	25%	15%
Protesting discrimination against Negroes in the armed services	3	7
Total of armed-service stories..	28%	22%

Underlying the armed-service stories, sometimes mentioned, always implied, was the familiar theme: if a Black is good enough to die for his country, why isn't he good enough to have an equal status with all other citizens?

The lag of the Black press can be traced to their inadequacy of news sources. The newspapers have suffered from the lack of an organized promotional service for creating big news. Only in the last two years has one or two newspapers launched individual efforts to make news. The Pittsburgh *Courier* has often checked on news stories reported by the Associated Press and proved them to be inaccurate. The *Courier* made important news when the newspaper cleared up a false report that Black baseball team owners were taking action against Branch

Rickey of the Brooklyn Dodgers for signing up Jackie Robinson, Black player—the first ever to receive a contract from one of the major league teams.

In the national capitol the Black press has never had representation in the galleries and therefore this firsthand source for political and legislative news has been closed to them. The newspapermen's applications have been turned down on the pretense that they could not meet the rigid requirements of the galleries. This is hardly true since many of the newspapers were in a financial position to maintain a representative to give full time servicing news by wire. The white Washington correspondents varied in their attitudes about admitting a Black member. Two widely known correspondents were said to be determined to block acceptance of a Black member. The standing committee that considers applications would probably be unable to reject the newsman on the grounds of color, and so subtle evasion and flimsy reasons were given for their rejection of the Black's applications.

Although Black newspaper reporters have been admitted to White House conferences since Calvin Coolidge's administration, this did not make up for the bar to the galleries. C. Lucien Skinner was the first Black newsman to attend White House conferences regularly and Louis R. Lantier was the second.

Perhaps Ted Poston, on the staff of the Office of War Information during World War II, did more than anyone in opening up new sources of news for the Black newspapers.

The majority of the Black newspapers were serviced by the Associated Negro Press, founded in 1919 by Claude A. Barnett and the late Nathum D. Brasher. Mimeographed releases were furnished to the newspapers, which would buy the service, three times weekly and in case of important news, telegrams were sent.

In the last few years some Black newspapers have expanded their news coverage and in a cooperative effort between many of the papers a wire service was developed. Fleming observed that

Negro papers are trying to do a better news covering job for their readers. The *Afro-American* sent its star reporter by air to Mississippi . . . to get first hand facts in lynching and

176

then followed that by sending him to the coronation of King George VI for those stories which the Associated Press and daily papers would not carry.

The Pittsburgh *Courier* sent J. A. Rogers, the historian, to Ethiopia during the Italian invasion; the New York *Amsterdam News* had its own correspondent at the Olympics; the Kansas City *Call, Afro-American,* and the *Amsterdam News,* Norfolk *Journal and Guide,* and the Philadelphia *Tribune* had two of their best writers from their joint staffs at the Decatur trial of the Scottsboro boys, who by wire and mail covered every angle of the case; the *Amsterdam News* used short wave radio, and other papers sent staff writers to cover the 1937 Ohio Valley floods; several papers maintain writers in Washington . . .

During the war, Black correspondents were sent by their newspapers to the various theaters of war. And among the two thousand reporters from all over the world at the San Francisco Conference to set up the United Nations Organization was a host of Black newsmen. The (Los Angeles) *Sentinel* covered the conference with great detail and reported special interviews with colored leaders of the world.

Many of the newspapers have dug into problems that relate primarily to Blacks through columnists. They have also attempted to broaden their readers' understanding of social conditions that involve our whole society. For instance the *Courier* and the *Defender* have white commentators.

Besides the expansion of editorial content that is calculated to inform, interpret, and crusade, the Black press has adopted a *Credo.* And when each tenet has been achieved securely by the individual members of this important group, the Black newspapers will no longer represent a "lag"—they will and should lead America to understand the real meaning of democracy.